STORIES of The OLD DUCK HUNTERS

&

OTHER DRIVEL

STORIES of The OLD DUCK HUNTERS

&

OTHER DRIVEL

by
GORDON
MacQUARRIE

compiled and edited by
ZACK TAYLOR

Published in 1979 by Willow Creek Press.

Copyright © 1967 by

THE STACKPOLE COMPANY

Cameron & Kelker Streets, Harrisburg, Pa. 17105

Library of Congress Catalogue Card Number: 67-12929

Printed in the U.S.A.

ISBN 0-932558-10-0

This book is dedicated to Ted Kesting who in more ways than one made it possible.

Contents

Introduction

Quite a few years ago now, a young Associate Editor on the magazine came into my office carrying a manuscript. "What has this guy got," he asked, "that nobody else has got?" I knew that another story by Gordon MacQuarrie had arrived.

I had been a member of the MacQuarrie fan club for a number of years by then. I had, in fact, come to the field only a short while after he started writing. He was one of the first I reached out for to produce the kind of outdoor writing and reporting I wanted in *Sports Afield*. There isn't any question that he along with a handful of others dramatized the needs of conservation, uplifted the whole approach to the outdoors, and popularized a new kind of reason to hunt and fish. To put it more simply: He helped make the outdoors as we know it today.

So no one could be more delighted than I that the Associate Editor finally got around to answering his own question. The editor was, of course, Zack Taylor. And the stories here, amplified by Zack's able introductions, are ample proof that time has in no way dimmed the quality that Gordon MacQuarrie had and shared with no other.

TED KESTING
Editor of Sports Afield

Gordon MacQuarrie

Gordon MacQuarrie was born in Superior, Wisconsin, July 3, 1900. He died November 10, 1956 in Milwaukee of a heart attack, his first real illness. He was the son of William MacQuarrie and Mary Elizabeth Stevenson MacQuarrie. Both the Stevenson and MacQuarrie families were Scottish in origin and had come to the United States by way of Canada.

He was graduated from Superior Central High School and attended the Superior State Teachers College for two years before attending the University of Wisconsin where he received a degree in journalism in 1923. He earned his way through college as a drummer with a dance band which played in the northern Wisconsin-Minnesota-Michigan area, and around the state university at Madison.

Upon graduation MacQuarrie joined the *Superior Evening Telegram* as a reporter. After two years he became city editor, and in 1927 managing editor. He left Superior in April 1936 to become outdoor editor of the *Milwaukee Journal*. He had been a guest columnist for the *Journal* and was widely known through stories in the leading sportsmen's magazines. He continued with the *Journal* for 20 years, a popular and prominent figure.

He was married to Helen Peck in 1927. She was the daughter of Al Peck, a Superior automobile dealer, who became the model for the first President of the Old Duck Hunters' Association, a fictitious organization MacQuarrie invented for literary purposes, although the two men actually were close and frequent companions. [MacQuarrie's first wife died in 1952. They had one daughter, the present Mrs. T. H. Wieder.]

After the death of Al Peck, the Old Duck Hunter series was discontinued for several years until a close attachment was formed with Mr. Harry Nohr, postmaster of Mineral Point, Wisconsin. He became the second Mr. President and the series was continued until 1956.

During his years with the *Journal*, MacQuarrie traveled an estimated 40,000 miles a year covering his special field. He developed an immense personal following with his unique blend of information and entertainment.

Northwest Wisconsin remained his favorite area and the scene of most of the Old Duck Hunter stories. It was there on the Eau Claire chain of lakes that his father, a carpenter for the Superior school system, built a log cabin while Mac-Quarrie was still in his teens. In the early days it was a sixteen-mile walk to the cabin from the nearest railroad stop. The cabin became his lifelong retreat, figuring in many of his stories.

In 1953, MacQuarrie married Ellen Gibson, then a reporter for the *Journal*.

Physically, he was a wiry, red-headed man with a down-to-earth attitude and a quick, salty wit. He entered the field of outdoor writing when it was at a low point; most stories were poorly written, with little or no imagination. With his light humor, careful character delineation, story sense, and descriptive ability he helped raise the level of the entire field. He was a pioneer, and a dedicated conservationist when it was neither fashionable nor politic to be one.

This is the first of the famous stories of the Old Duck Hunters' Association, Inc.—"Inc." standing for "Incorrigible." It was written many years after the actual event. In it MacQuarrie, an accomplished fisherman and upland shooter, recalls his introduction to duck shooting by his father-in-law.

By the time this was written MacQuarrie was at the top of his field. His job as outdoor editor on a leading newspaper in an enthusiastic outdoor state gave him great prominence and knowledge. His technical articles on all phases of the outdoors appeared regularly in all the outdoor magazines. But with it all, for the man, there was something lacking.
It wasn't enough.

MacQuarrie felt the need to make some deep statements about the outdoors. What it should mean to people. What it could do for people. He couldn't have known it at the time but the Old Duck Hunter stories were to become the vehicle that enabled him to do this and more. For almost 20 years, as MacQuarrie the writer and the man matured, his interpretations of the outdoors, told with unforgettable zest and humor, went far beyond humor to come to grips with life; what to get out of it, and what it means.

1

"Ducks? You Bat You!"

Tonight is the end of summer. A needle-fine rain is pelting the shingles. Autos swish by on wet concrete. Until now summer has been in full command. This full, cold rain is the first harbinger of autumn.

Maybe the cold rain started me off. A flood of recollections of my first duck-hunting trip crowds everything else from my mind. Just such a rain—only colder—was falling from northern Wisconsin skies that night in late October, many years ago, when the President of the Old Duck Hunters' Association, Inc., rapped at my door.

It was an impatient rap. I found him standing in the hall, quizzical, eager, in his old brown mackinaw that later was to become his badge of office. As always, only a top button of the mackinaw was fastened. His brown felt hat dripped rain. Below the sagging corners of the mackinaw were high tan rubber boots. He danced a brief jig, partly to shake off the rain and partly to celebrate an impending duck hunt.

"Hurry up!" he said.

"Where?"

"You're going duck hunting."

That was news. I had never been duck hunting. Not once in a varied life devoted to fishing and hunting had I ever hunted ducks. For some reason, ducks had not appealed to me. They had been just something that flew over a lake where I was fishing late in the year. I didn't know it then, but I was much like a person who has grown to maturity without having read "Robinson Crusoe."

"Shut the door!" a voice cried from within my house.

It was my wife, the daughter of the President, the only person who awes Mr. President. He shuffled through the door with alacrity and took a tongue-lashing for sprinkling water on the floor.

"Who's going duck hunting?" demanded the lady, adding, "And who says who can go duck hunting? Isn't it enough that he spends all his idle moments fishing?"

"It's like this," began Hizzoner. "I told him last summer that now, since he was more or less one of the family, I ought to take him duck hunting. He's been at our house eating ducks and currant jam for years. Why shouldn't he contribute to the—er—groaning board?"

"I see," said the daughter of the President cannily. "You want someone to row the boat."

"I do not!" he replied indignantly. "I even borrowed a gun for him."

"You'll find he won't row. He won't even put up curtain rods. He looks like a dead loss for both of us."

"I'll take a chance on him."

From a closet she helped me resurrect heavy clothing, including an old sheepskin coat. When I was ready, the President advised his only heir that he would return the body safely some time the next evening. It was then about 8 P.M. The lady whom I had wed only some four months previously sat down resignedly with a magazine. Her parting injunction was: "Mallards. Get some mallards."

A loaded car was at the curb. Wedged in a corner of the back seat beside duffel and a crate of live duck decoys was a huge figure that answered to the name of Fred. Later I was to learn that better duck shots have seldom displayed their wares on any of our local waters.

Down sandy highway No. 35 with the rain streaking the windshield, off to the right at the store in Burnett County, over the humpbacked hills, then into a yard beyond which a light from a house gleamed among huge oak trees. As we drove up, a floodlight came on, as though someone within the house had been waiting for us.

It was Norm. Always there is a Norm for duck hunters who really mean it, some vigilant sentinel of the marshes who phones to say, "The flight is in." Norm was apprehensive. As we stored things in our allotted cabin we did not have to be reminded by him that it was growing colder. The rain was abating, and a northwest wind was rocking the oaks. "Little Bass may be frozen over," said Norm. "You should have come when I first phoned, two days ago. The temperature has fallen from 55 to 40 since sunset."

We occupied the cabin. There were two full-sized beds. Norm built up a roaring jack-pine fire in the little air-tight stove. There was much palaver along instructional lines for my benefit. Later my two benefactors prepared for bed.

"We'll give you the single bed," said the President magnanimously. "Fred and I are used to sleeping together. We'll put this extra blanket between the beds. Whoever gets cold and needs it can just reach over for it. Good-night."

In five minutes they were asleep. Outside the wind rose. Even before I fell asleep, only half warm, I contemplated the probability of grabbing that blanket. Later I woke. I was somewhat congealed. I reached for the blanket. It was gone. I tried to fall asleep without it, but the cold was steadily growing worse.

Teeth chattering, I got up, lit a kerosene lamp and discovered the blanket carefully tucked around the two sleeping forms in the other bed. Sound asleep and snoring gently lay my two kind old friends. I wouldn't for the world snake that blanket off their aging bones. Not me!

I piled all available clothing on top my own thin blanket

and tried again to sleep. At times I almost succeeded, but it
was along toward 3:30 A.M. when I got up, lit a fire in the
stove and thawed out. Then I dozed in an old rocking chair,
to be awakened soon by a loud thumping on the single wall
of the cabin.

It was Norm delivering his summons to his hunters. I
turned up the wick on the lamp. The President and Fred
awakened languorously. The President sat upright, threw his
legs over the edge of the bed and studied the top of the table
where the blanket had rested.

"Just looking for scratches in the varnish," he said.
"Dreamed last night I heard someone reaching for that
blanket. Wasn't you, was it? Surely a young man with your
abounding vitality wouldn't be needing an extra blanket?"

"Why, we've got the blanket ourselves," chimed in Fred.
"Now isn't that funny? Do you know, I had a dream too.
Dreamed I was cold in the night and got up and took the
derned blanket."

Since then I have learned to get that extra blanket in a
hurry.

In Norm's kitchen there was a beaming platter of eggs
and bacon. When it was empty, the platter was refilled with
sour-cream pancakes, such as people often talk about but
seldom can get. And after that a big white coffee pot was
passed around as the Old Duck Hunters', Inc., washed down
layer after layer of toast.

Outside it was bitter cold. The first real arctic blast had
helped to dry the sand roads. Where it did not dry them
the cold froze them, so that the car lurched and bumped
along the ruts. There was the faintest hint of dawn as the
car turned through a cornfield, plunged over rough ground
a hundred yards and came to a stop near the base of a long
point thrusting into the middle of a narrow, shallow lake.

This point on Little Bass Lake was—and still is—one of the
most sought-after ducking points in northwest Wisconsin.

Situated north of Big Yellow, this shallow lake with its swampy shores is a natural haven for ducks escaping bombardment on the bigger lake.

From a near-by patch of scrub-oak the President hauled at something until, in the faint light, I saw he had hold of a duck boat. I helped him drag it to the water. He paddled off through thin ice inshore to spread the decoys in open water. While he was busy at this morning ritual the searing slash of duck wings came down to us a half dozen times. Fred called to him to hurry, but no one hurries the President when he is making a set.

Finally he came ashore and occupied the small scrub-oak blind alongside mine. Even then he was not content to sit and wait, as was Fred in the near-by blind, but counted over and over again the wooden decoys. And was dissatisfied when he had thirty-two. "Anyone knows you've got to have an uneven number. Why, thirteen is better than any even number!" he chafed.

I just sat. Said I to myself, "So this is duck hunting." Just sit and wait.

Then there was a searing roar in back of us. I was about to raise my head to see what it was, but the mittened hand of Mr. President seized my shoulder and pulled me down to the sand floor of the blind. He himself seemed to be groveling in the sand, and from the nearby cover where Fred skulked I heard him stage-whisper: "Don't move. They're flying in back to look us over."

Twice again the sound of many wings cleaving the frosty air was borne down to us. At no time did I dare look up. The sound faded, disappeared entirely, then swelled again, louder and louder. When it seemed it could grow no louder, it changed to a hissing diminuendo. That sound was my first introduction to the music of stiff, set wings on a long glide down.

"Now!" Maybe it was Fred who said it, maybe it was Mr. President.

Before I had thrust my head over the parapet of scrub-oak Fred's 32-inch double had sounded and the President, who shot a pump in those days, had fired once and was grunting and straining to operate the action for the next shot. He had to catch that old corn-sheller of his just right to make it throw the empty out and a new shell in. Always, whether it worked smoothly or not, the President gave off a groaning, whining sound between shots, like an angry terrier held back from a square meal. He got off three shots before I could make out a low-flying squad of dark objects hightailing across the lake.

"Bluebills," said the President.

On the open water beyond the rushes and in the quieter water on the very thin ice were five objects. I dragged the duck boat from its thicket and retrieved them. One of them had green on its wings. "What the—?" said Fred. "Look, Al! One greenwing among those bluebills."

So this was duck hunting. Well, not bad. Not bad at all. Indeed not!

The sounds of swift wings and booming guns were good sounds. The smell of burned powder was a good smell. The feel of those birds, warm in a bare hand, was a good feeling. My toes had been cold; now they were tingling. I knew those five ducks would go best with wild rice and currant jelly. They made a nice little pile at our feet in the blind.

After a while Gus Blomberg, who owned the point and lived in a little house five hundred yards back of us, came down through the oaks to see what was going on. He took a chew of snuff and said: "Halloo-o-o! How iss it, eh? Nice docks, you bat you!"

Great guy, Gus. Fred gave him a dollar. That was for the use of his point. Gus said "Tenk you," and also, "How 'bout leetle coffee at noon, eh? Goes good cold day. You bat you!"

Gus went away. The President stood up occasionally and beat his mitts together to warm his fingers. Fred just sat. He had enough fat to keep him warm. I never saw him wear gloves in a blind, even on frightfully cold December mornings. All Fred wore was his old shooting jacket and a cigarette. He could keep his cigarette lit in a cloudburst.

Other ducks came in. Some went on, and some stayed. After a while it occurred to me that I might try a shot at a duck myself.

"Haven't you had your gun here all this time?" asked the President. And he meant it; he had been too busy to think of anything but that early-morning flight. He took me back to the car and unearthed a short-barreled hammer-lock, the fore piece of which was held firm by close-wrapped wire.

"It's the best I could find around the neighborhood," he said. "The choke has been sawed off. Don't shoot at anything unless it's on top of you."

So I had a gun. This duck-hunting business was getting better and better.

Back in the blind, Fred had a couple more down. A flock of four bluebills came in. They were trusting souls. They neither circled nor hesitated. They came spang in, from straight out in front, low. They set their wings. I picked out one and fired—both barrels. One fell at the second shot.

My first duck! Lying out there on the thin ice, white breast up, dead as a door-nail. The President and Fred had declined to shoot. They were furthering the education of a novice. They were, in fact, letting the duck-hunting virus take full effect. They laughed at me and pounded me on the back and kidded me, and all day after that they seemed to get an awful kick out of just looking at me and grinning.

About noon it began to snow. The wind fell off. The decoys froze in tightly. Fred stirred and said, "Coffee!" Hizzoner explained to me that it was necessary to pull in the blocks before leaving the blind. I was glad for the exercise.

After coffee and some of the other things had been duly consumed, we returned to the blind, Fred to his motionless waiting. Hizzoner to his quick, bird-like neck craning. The President usually saw the ducks first and signaled Fred. It did not perturb Fred much. The only sign of excitement from him was a gradual drawing-in of his neck, turtle-like. Then he would stamp out the last quarter-inch of his cigarette and wait. At the crucial moment he didn't stand to fire; he just straightened out his legs and sort of rared up. He was by far the best duck shot I have ever seen.

Maybe I killed another duck; I am not sure. From then on I shot with the others. They had let me have my chance. I had killed a duck. It had been an easy shot. They knew that. So did I. But they did not speak of it. They just kept grinning, for they must have known I had been ordained to love the game and they were glad to help a natural destiny work itself out.

They grinned when I threw myself into the small chores that beset the duck hunter. Dragging the duck boat from the thicket for a pick-up, cutting new boughs for the blind, walking around the sedgy shore of Little Bass to pick up a cripple that had drifted over, driving back for a package of cigarettes for Fred.

To all these tasks I set myself eagerly. They came as part of the game. Those two rascals had frozen me the night before; but they had introduced me to something new and something good, and I was grateful.

Since then, while hunting with these two I have felt this obligation to do my part. Both are many years older than I, and they have appreciated it, but, of course, never mentioned it. They would prefer to guy me with mild rebuke, criticize my shooting and otherwise continue the good work already well begun.

Of such stuff are the recollections of that first ducking trip. Diverse images, grateful peeks back at two wise and capable practitioners of what has become for me the most dramatic thing in outdoor sports.

The outdoors holds many things of keen delight. A deer flashing across a burn, a squirrel corkscrewing up a tree trunk, a sharptail throbbing up from the stubble—all these have their place in my scheme of things. But the magic visitation of ducks from the sky to a set of bobbing blocks holds more of beauty and heart-pounding thrill than I have ever experienced afield with rod or gun. Not even the sure, hard pluck of a hard-to-fool brown trout, or the lurching smash of a river smallmouth has stirred me as has the circling caution of ducks coming to decoys.

The afternoon wore on. Shortly before quitting time Gus came back, to stand with Fred for a chance at a few mallards. He took a brace and was satisfied. Mr. President said he thought he'd take a walk around the north end of Little Bass "just for the fun of it." Gus said he might find a mallard or two if there was open water, "but you got to sneak opp on dem. You bat!"

"You bat you, too, Gus," said the President. He buttoned the second button on the brown mackinaw and headed into the swirling flakes.

Fred lit a cigarette. We waited. Collars and mittens were now soggy with snow water. Fred's magic cigarette somehow managed to stay lit and in the waning light glowed more brightly. From the north end of the lake came four reports, muffled by the distance and the snow.

"Ay hope iss dem mollard," said Gus. "Al, he like dem mollard, you bat you!"

We were picked up and packed up when the President returned. The President had two mallards, of course. He dropped them in the car trunk with the other birds and unbuttoned the top button of the old brown mackinaw. We stood in the snow and said good-by to Gus. Added to his brace of birds were three more that Fred gave him. He turned and walked away through the rasping corn-stalks with a final, "You bat you!"

The President addressed me: "How'd you like it?"

In those days I was very young. It took me a long time to try to say what I felt. I have never succeeded yet. I simply babbled.

We drove out of the cornfield, stopped to yell good-by to Norm, who came out to his back door to wave, and then headed for the main highway. I drove. Fred reposed in the back, comfortable as the clucking ducks against whose crate he leaned. At my side sat the President. The light from the cowl partly illuminated his strong, sharp features.

Finally I said: "Wish you had let me in on this earlier in the season. There won't be another duck week-end after today."

The President flicked cigar ashes and replied: "I thought of that, but decided to break it to you gently. Too much of a good thing is bad for a growing boy."

*"Get ready, my friend. I am just brushing
by to settle the dust and wash away today's
dead spent-wings."*

*With these words, the author gives fair
warning that bigger game than ducks and deer
are to be hunted on the pages that lie ahead.
Laughter and love will be the bullets to down
the elusive targets. And while hundreds of
minds greater than the self-admitted puerile
brains of the ODHA, Inc. have blanched before
such an awesome assignment, rest assured the
two-man membership is in no way dismayed.
There is always Mr. President. A most
undismayable man.*

*MacQuarrie, in his personal life, was growing
closer to this man with "sharp brown eyes, a
mouth on the upturned quizzical side, horn-
rimmed glasses, a goodly swath of gray in the
black hair." He might have been any other
harassed slave of commerce. But about this
one, "there was something of the boy which
most men pretend to outgrow, and doing
so, thus become old."*

*As the stories go past you will be moved
and warmed by the deepening relationship
between the old man and his acquired son.
It alone is worth the price of admission.*

*But Mr. President will soon come to symbolize
and portray much that MacQuarrie felt about
the outdoors. There is a long and adventurous
journey ahead. A companion is essential. He
must be indefatigable and expert. A man of
great energy and enthusiasm. By all rights he
should be a sober, ponderous, God-fearing
soul. But this one happens to be full of the
devil. Incomparable. Incorrigible. Delightful!*

2

Upon the
Earth Below

There is something about rain. . . . At night in summer when the clouds can swell no more and shrink from threatening battlements to ragged shreds over Wisconsin, I often get up from my chair, go to the big closet and speculate over the implements of trout fishing there. Indeed, there is something about rain. Especially a warm rain, spilled over a city or a network of trout streams. It kindles a spark. It presses a button. It is an urgent message from afar to any seeker of the holy grail of anglingdom—trout.

There is the mild August rain sluicing down to the thirsty earth. There are the castellated clouds, fresh from the Western prairie, borne on the hot, dry land wind. And there is your man of the creel and the throbbing rod and the sodden waders going to the window to peer out and plumb the mysteries of the rain and wonder about tomorrow.

It must be that aeons ago, when the rain splashed down over the front of a cave door, the muscle-bound troglodyte within went to the opening and stretched out his hand, palm upward. Perhaps he even stood in it a bit, as perfectly sane men will sometimes do. Perhaps that old sprig of Adam, restless by his fire in the dry cave, felt the friendliness of the rain. Perhaps—no troutster will deny it—he felt the drops upon his matted head and wondered about tomorrow.

27

The rain can beckon a man of the noisy city and draw him to the door or window. Its attraction is so much the greater if it falls at night, when it is a whispering mystic visitor from afar that seems to say: "Get ready, my friend. I am just brushing by to settle the dust and wash away today's dead spent-wings."

One night I was sitting alone, restless behind my newspaper. The rain had barely begun. I was feeling its pull. Dark had just fallen, and the rain had come tentatively, like a guest afraid of a cool welcome. It had grown darker, and the rain came stronger. I cast the paper aside and went to the door.

All of the lush buoyance of August was in the night wind that came through the screen. To my nostrils came the scent of wet turf, and in the sparkling lines of rain that penciled down in the porch light I seemed to see the exuberant waters where the trout dwell.

I stared out. The lightning flashed on and off. Two pine trees by my door tossed and glistened. I was lost there for minutes contemplating the beauty of the night.

Also, I knew what the rain would do for certain trout waters. Some of them it would raise; some would even go over their banks. Others, mothered by heavily grown forest country, would take up the water slowly. The trout would be grateful, as it had been dry and hot for a long time. There would be new feed in the streams tomorrow.

From my dry vestibule, nose pressed to the screen, over which hung a small protecting porch roof, I made out, in one lightning flash, the figure of a man. He was walking slowly and deliberately in the downpour. He came across the street under the corner light, and at the distance of fifty yards I could see that the water had flattened the brim of his hat.

He vanished into darkness, walking toward me. Here, I said, is a man doing what I would wish to do if I didn't give a rip about the crease in these trousers. A man out shaking hands with an August rainstorm. I enjoyed his enjoyment.

I could almost feel the warm drops cascading off my nose, the squishing of my shoes and the cool touch of rain on my cheeks.

He came closer, passing the mountain ash trees near my walk, sloshing as slowly and happily as ever. And then, as though he had seen me, he turned up my walk. It was not until he strode into the wan light of the tiny porch that I recognized him—the President of the Old Duck Hunters' Association.

He stood beyond the porch roof in the drip, grinning in at me. "This is it," he said.

"And you're fixing to catch a dandy summer cold. Come in."

He stamped off some of the drops, dashed the water from his soaking hat and sized me up. "A little rain," he lectured, "never hurt anyone. Especially a fisherman. This is exactly what these August trout streams have been waiting for."

I lured him inside.

"How about tomorrow?" he said.

I was not given an opportunity to accept his invitation. He rushed on.

"It's close to the end of the month now. This will be the last warm rain of the season. Next good one we get will be a cold September drizzle. Wait and see. Better get that trout fishin' done while there's time. A trout has got to have new rain every so often. . . ."

In the living room the situation hit me differently. The spell of the storm had left me, and now all I could think of was Mister President, dripping on my newly covered davenport, selling me a bill of fishing goods. I laughed. It must have seemed a smug laugh to him, such a laugh as a non-venturesome, dry-shod city prisoner would get off in the presence of a dyed-in-the-wool trout fisherman.

"Laugh and be danged," he snorted. "I'll walk five more blocks in this very fine rainstorm to the door of a real fisherman, and I'll bet you anything he'll not only come along with me tomorrow, but he'll walk home with me in the rain— without an umbrella."

I capitulated, of course. It is always good wisdom to capitulate to a President of the Old Duck Hunters. I even offered him dry socks and a hot drink and spread his dripping jacket in front of the gas oven. He sat there for a long spell, talking trout, and when his warming drink was finished he strode back into the night, to walk like a man and a trout fisherman in the friendly element.

It was not until the next afternoon that I plumbed his further thoughts about the rain. I wanted to get the whole of his philosophy of tramping through a downpour. I sensed a little of it, but wanted to learn more of what stirs the depths of such as he.

"It's like this," he said, shifting his cigar and leaning over the steering wheel which was guiding us to the Iron River, in north Wisconsin. "Up to yesterday it hadn't rained in weeks. I was getting as dry as your hollyhocks. Every day had been the same. Bright, dazzling sun, same old grind in the office. Monotony.

"Then it rained. I was working late. I watched that storm gather, and the heavier the clouds came in from the west the better I felt. Do you suppose there's anything to this here theory that a little electricity in the air peps up a fellow? I kept working through the rain, getting more done than I had all day. And when I was through I said, 'Now for a good walk in the rain.' Why? I just wanted to. The reason I came to your house first was so I could dry off some before my wife saw me."

I didn't quite get it yet.

He continued: "Don't you ever feel like plunging into a snowstorm, or wading a tough river, or climbing a hill? Maybe it's a way of letting off steam. Or maybe I've fished trout so long I'm getting just like a trout, rushing out from under the bank in a rain to see what the river is bringing down for supper. Could be."

I looked him over. A lean, keen business man, much like many another business man except for the fisherman's garb. Sharp brown eyes, a mouth on the upturned quizzical side, horn-rimmed glasses, a goodly swath of gray in the black hair. Yes, he might have been any other harassed slave of commerce on a fishing recess, but he was not. There was something of the boy about him which most men pretend to outgrow, and, doing so, thus become old.

We drove to the Iron in bright sun, and the President stuffed his faded khaki fishing jacket with the things he would need. He donned waders, rigged up, applied mosquito dope, and, with a final flourish, adjusted the old brown fishing felt with the hook-marred band. Then he was gone, leaving me to climb into gear and ruminate upon a way of life that brings a man to an even three-score with the heart of a boy.

I got into the Iron at a little meadow-like spot not far from Wisconsin's Highway 13. The sun was high. Last night's rain had hardly raised the stream. There was a freshness in the woods that all trout fishermen will recall—the freshness of soaking turf and rain-washed air, and the silver tinkling of a wren and the sweet lament of a white-throated sparrow. I hardly feel that I have been trout fishing if I do not hear this precious bird along the stream.

Things went indifferently for an hour. Fish were rising, but they were the tiny, ubiquitous rainbows, so common in streams that empty into Lake Superior and so laughably pugnacious, coming out to smash a fly like a feather-weight sparring with Joe Louis.

By four o'clock the outdoor stage was being set as it was the previous evening. The black, bulbous clouds in the west, borne into Wisconsin by the day-long prairie wind, were rumbling and flickering distantly. I knew it was only a matter of minutes before the storm would be over the Iron.

But it was a fine time to fish. As the first drops fell I got into a fair rainbow, creeled it and went on hastily, to search other likely corners. From a grassy place in midstream came a big enough brown, enticed out of its scant cover by the lure of new food. Downstream a bit I took two more rainbows. All came to a very, very wet single Royal Coachman.

A wind came out of those plumbeous clouds that stirred the popples joyously, so that their long-stemmed leaves turned upward and revealed the silver gray of their under sides. I could feel the rain going through canvas and flannel to my shoulders. The river was boiling like a kettle. "Fine," said I. Trout were out in it. The President was out in it. I was out in it. Let it come. I looked back, and there, a hundred yards downstream, was the President, hailing me.

"Hurry up!" he yelled.

I went to him. He was certainly in a hurry. He had his rod taken down, but the line was still strung through the guides.

"Got to get out of here quick," he said. He was short of breath. He had hurried to locate me.

"Get out of here?"

"And I mean right now—clay roads!"

I hadn't thought of that. I got to the car ahead of him. I was remembering stalled cars in Lake Superior's red clay and one nightmare exit from a similar spot where he and I made it out only by wrapping wool socks around the wheels in lieu of chains.

No time to climb out of waders. The rain was sluicing down. We had one chance of getting out of that clay-road country to graveled highway. It lay in the fact that we would be the first ones over the sharply crowned road on which we had come in. We might, by luck and careful driving, bite down with our tires and get hold of traction.

It was nip and tuck. But we made it, thanks to the skillful tooling of Mister President, who is an old hand with slippery clay roads. There were a couple of little hogbacks, however, that we actually slid down.

On the graveled road, he drew up at the side and switched off the motor. It was around 4:30 by then. He pawed around in the back seat and came up with sandwiches and coffee. Studying the rain-dashed windshield, he made more trout medicine.

"We'll go back to the Brule, in by George Yale's at Rainbow Bend, and have one more fling at it. Won't have to worry about roads there."

Further trout fishing had been far from my mind, but just when you think the President is in a corner he wriggles out and starts a new campaign. "No hurry," he pointed out. "Sit there and finish your coffee—and here, sit on this old raincoat. I can't have you ruining the upholstery on a new $1,800 automobile."

Ruin the upholstery! Heck, I had been with him in the scrub-oak country one day when those tough-tipped branches made an $1,800 job look as if it had been sandpapered. He wasn't concerned. He was more concerned about two limits of mallards we had taken that day from a hard-to-get-at pot-hole.

"About seven o'clock will be soon enough to hit the Brule," he ventured. "Just a half hour or hour is all I want. A few good ones ought to be out by then."

We sat and talked. We even had time, between showers, to straighten out some of our hastily stowed tackle, and the heat of our bodies partially dried our upper clothing. We talked as do all trout fishermen confined in an auto—of politics and making money and how to get along with one's neighbors and fishing for trout and waiting in frosty duck blinds at dawn.

Fed and reorganized, we drove slowly south and a bit west to the Brule at Rainbow Bend. It is a favorite putting-in place for the confirmed wader. On the peak of land which juts out into this enticing stream in front of the forest ranger's

house we sat for more minutes and watched the sun go down
behind threatening clouds. By then it had stopped raining.
The President lit a fresh cigar and studied the clouds from
the west.

"It'll rain again," he predicted.

Darkness was coming fast. The woods dripped. A few
between-the-rain mosquitoes were venturing forth. A whippoorwill sent out an exploratory note.

"What time shall we meet at the car?"

"I don't like this fishing in the dark myself," he explained.
"Let's fish for an hour and call it a day."

At this place, where the pines lean over the Brule, he
jointed his rod and was off down the path on the right bank.

I put in above the Ranger's station, intending to fish above
the old stone dam in a stretch that I respect most highly for
its combination of quite fast water and long, deep holes. In
late summer when aerated water is preferred by trout, I have
found this place to be excellent.

Such evenings are long remembered. Nighthawks swooped
and cried above me as I went slowly upstream on the right
bank. Before I got to my beginning point my neck and
shoulders were soaked again from dripping trees.

It was still light enough to hold the eye of a fly to the
graying sky and thread a 1X leader through it. I like this
place. I have been very lucky here. I leaned against a great
rock while I tied on a floater and studied for the hundredth
time the familiar stairway of rapids which lay before me.

One of the best things about trout fishing is going back to
a familiar place. Then the woods welcome a man. It is not
like being alone on a strange river.

I worked out line over the wavelets at the foot of my
rapids, but turned over nothing more than the omnipresent
baby rainbows. Hugging the right bank and working farther
into the hard flow of this swift water, I did better across in
the slack water of the left bank when an 11-inch brown,

tempted by a back-circling bivisible in an eddy, smacked it hard and sure.

Very well. They were out on the prod, following the rain as Mister President had judged they would be. They seemed everywhere in that foaming water. And they were not choosy. It was dark enough to invite them to be impetuous, and light enough to make for agreeable fishing.

The fish of that place I remember was a stout brown. It came out of the swiftest water in mid-current, seized the fly and went downstream, all in one swoop. With a four-ounce rod and a 1X leader in that kind of water a solid fish like this one, below a man, has all the advantage. I stumbled downstream after him, played him out in the slack water and slipped him in the rubber pocket of my jacket. I thought then that he might go 18 inches. Anyway, I decided, I would claim that length before Mister President.

By squinting a bit I made out the time—8:30. The hour was up. I returned to the car in the pines on the hill, put everything carefully away, examined the buster trout gloatingly in the car headlights and composed myself behind the wheel to wait for Mister President. Off in the west there was hardly enough daylight remaining to backlight the pointed spruce tops. Back of me and over me the sky was invisible. A big drop of rain hit the windshield hard. I sensed what was coming.

There was a pause in the small night sounds of the Brule valley. I listened. From far off came the bold, surging roar of rain on leaves. The sound came nearer, rushing through the woods in an ear-filling crescendo. Then the rain hit.

It made a goodly cascade on the windshield. It hammered at the steel car top. It was a million wet drumsticks on the hood. With it came a wild, quick wind, whooping and screaming through the tree-tops. The lights, switched on, revealed steel-bright pencils of rain.

Too bad. The President was down in that rain-stricken

valley somewhere getting soaked anew. He might have escaped a second wetting had he quit the stream at the appointed time. He might have been sitting there with me in the dry front seat, looking out into it.

I was feeling pretty smug about it. The President is a late-stayer. This time, I thought, he was going to pay the penalty for not keeping an appointment. And then there was that damp, comforting lump in the rubber-lined pocket. I could feel it by reaching a hand down over the back of the seat to where my jacket lay on the floor.

I would take my time about showing him that one. I'd be nonchalant. I'd haul out the little ones first, wait for him to snort at them and then produce the good one. I'd show him. I'd say it was a wonder a man can't depend on his best friend's word. I'd say that when I tell a fellow I'll meet him at such and such a time I meet him then, and don't keep him waiting in a cloudburst.

Time dragged. I am an impatient waiter. Would he ever return? A half hour passed. Then an hour. I turned on the lights from time to time at imaginary sounds from the path up which he would come. It was a long, boring, fretful wait.

Just after the legal quitting time of 10 P.M., I really did hear boots crunch against gravel. I switched the lights on to light his way, for it was Mister President. He came forward in the downpour. The old brown felt was sagging. He wore that unconcerned, listless air of a fisherman who is about to declare, "I gave 'em everything in the book, but they wouldn't play." I opened the car door, and he squished in. Played out, he demanded hot coffee and sipped it while listening to my evening's report.

He lighted up some at the sight of the 18-incher, but said it wouldn't go more than 15. "Maybe only 14½," he ventured. Nope, he hadn't a thing worth while. That dratted rain! And when it grew dark, he had his troubles in fighting the river without a flashlight. He wormed out of wet gear and into dry, gol-durning his luck and the weather. We prepared to drive home.

"I'll take down your rod," I offered, and went outside to where he had leaned it against a fender.

I hastily disjointed it and crawled back behind the wheel, handing the rod joints back to him. Then I discovered I was sitting on something. Something big and cold and wet. Something he had put in my place while I was getting the rod.

I turned around and stared down at the largest just-caught native brook trout I have seen come out of the Brule. Later it went a mite under four pounds—something of a miracle in this day and age, when all men know the big fish of the Brule are invariably browns or rainbows.

Hizzoner was chuckling now. The fish, he explained, hit a No. 4 brown fly that didn't have a name. He had heard it feeding in the dark and rain, and stayed with it for a half hour until it rose to the fly. He admitted it was the largest brookie he had ever taken in the Brule.

I stared at it as a man will stare at so rare a treasure. I envisioned the battle that took place down in that storm-lashed valley. The lightning must have seen a classic combat that night. I held the fish up and examined it by the dome light. "How long do you suppose it is?"

He snorted a triumphant snort from his throne in the rear and shot back: "Put it alongside that 18-incher of yours. The way you figger, it'll go just a yard long—just one yard!"

*MacQuarrie was on a plane with Ernest
Hemingway in his ability to impart the sensual
aspects of the outdoors. The sights, smells, and
emotions. Nowhere is that ability shown to
greater advantage than in the story
that follows.*

3

*There is greater significance here. "Just Look
at This Country" anticipates, years ahead of its
time, the direction the outdoor field is taking
today. Sportsmen are just beginning to understand and accept the fact that the era of
heavy bags and large kills is gone, just as the
need to hunt for food is no longer a part
of the world we know.*

*What replaces these ancient and worthy
motives? MacQuarrie answers this in what
is to become an ever-recurrent message,
one of his central themes.*

*"Perhaps here in an outdoor magazine
devoted to fishing, hunting and kindred sports,
is no place to confess hunting was secondary
out there in sun-drenched hills. Perhaps. But
I doubt it. What do those who ask why men
go hunting know of the tryst a hunting man
keeps with the wind and the trees and the sky?
Hunting? The means are greater than the
end and every deer hunter knows it."*

Just Look
at This Country

"Look at this country. Just look at it!" The words leaped up in me like that on the opening day of Wisconsin's deer season. I stood on the top of a high hill with a rifle in my hand and looked across miles of grand, rugged hunting country.

You've made that same exclamation yourself, perhaps at the end of a hard portage trail when a blue, spruce-girt lake opened before you. Or when you saw sweeping country below you at the end of a hard climb.

The sight of that Wisconsin wilderness made me feel like getting back in there for a prowl instead of proceeding to the immediate business of hunting deer. I had never seen this big, rough patch of Wisconsin before, although I had fished and hunted around its edges for years. It was like discovering a pearl in an oyster.

Thousands of acres of madly arranged hills. Some pyramidal, some cone-shaped. Snaky ridges with slopes ranging from steep to gentle. Little valleys and big valleys. None more than two hundred feet below the highest elevations. Some just pot-holes, round as the inside of an old kettle. Others long, V-shaped troughs.

Country like that makes me want to go look-see. I have a keener appreciation of what Kipling meant when he wrote: "Something lost behind the ranges, lost and waiting for you. Go!"

Our group included only three hunters. There was Dr. Patrick Tierney, a broth of a huntsman with a flair for far going. And there was that redoubtable, that peerless, that matchless gentleman and woodsman of the cut-over—the President of the Old Duck Hunters' Association, Inc.

The Tierney, a lithe-legged spalpeen, had been telling me about this country for years. When I looked at it—and kept on looking—there came over his face an expression of deep gratification such as his ancestors wore when they unveiled the Blarney stone. We stood and discussed it, Pat and I. His black Irish eyes snapped.

"I've hunted it for years," he said. "Sometimes I get my buck, sometimes not. I just like to get in there and travel."

The President of the Old Duck Hunters observed this meeting of Scotch and Irish minds with misgivings. He looked at the country, of course. He even tossed in a few superlatives of his own, but the tenor of his conversation was businesslike: "It looks like mighty tough going for a couple of old fellows like you and Pat."

He loaded his "far-reachin' " gun, a .38-55. Don't laugh, oh my brethren of the flat-shootin' stuff, for what reaches far for Mister President may not reach so far for Joe Doakes. As Pat said, eyeing the noble arm, "You can't tell from the looks of a frog how far he'll jump."

Then the President cleared his throat impatiently.

"Gentlemen," he began, "it's high noon of opening day. There is no snow. The sun is bright. I did not come here to listen to an oral survey of this hunk of God-forgotten sand. We'll drive, of course. There aren't enough of us to do it right, but we can get along. You two work west through the gullies, and I'll be over by that old rampike, waitin'."

We still surveyed the country, talking. The President said it was getting on and we hadn't yet seen anything with horns on it. Finally Pat made up his mind.

"Mister President," he said, "I am tired. I want to get more tired—a different kind of tired. I want to go out in those hills and walk my legs off, all by myself."

"You don't mean to say," snorted the President, "that you won't make even one little push through the alders?"

The drive is the thing in Wisconsin. The President—all of us, in fact—were brought up with deer hunters who drive. Still-hunting? Grand sport, indeed, but the rules are upset when 100,000 hunters go into the woods. I told the President I felt as Pat did: that I'd like nothing better than a long, hard swing through the hills. He was aghast.

"A couple of naturalists, eh?" he shot at us. "Going out to enjoy the beauties of nature. Sorry I didn't bring my wife along. She loves to gather wintergreen berries at this season!"

We protested. It wasn't that, exactly. It was just that a couple of city-pent fellows wanted to tramp the bush. He could hardly believe it. He waggled a finger under my nose and exploded: "I'd never have come if I'd known it! There are anyway a hundred bucks back in those hills. A little drive— nothing to it. We shouldn't settle for anything less than one today. It's opening day!"

We finally convinced him we preferred it our way, every man for himself. He moved quickly then. He pumped the cartridges out of the .38-55 and put the gun back in its case. He dived into my car and from its depths yelled: "Have you got that old pig-iron shotgun here?"

I had. It is an ancient arm, the open barrel of which will throw a shotgun slug about as accurately as your grand-mother would pitch 'em over at the Polo Grounds. But the choke barrel is accurate with slugs. I explained this to him. I explained further that it was an exceedingly temperamental cannon, given to letting off both barrels if you pulled the rear trigger. He said all he wanted was one crack at whatever he saw, because he was going to be almighty close to it. He dug in the inexhaustible pocket of the old brown mackinaw and found two 12-gauge slugs, pocket-worn but lethal.

Pat offered his .250-3000, but he declined. No, sir!

"As long as it's still-hunting with the cards stacked against you and the herd running wild everywhere, I'll take the elephant gun!"

He inspected the old shotgun. "I never shot one of these things at a deer in my life," he declared. "But you boys have put me on the spot. You've made an Indian out of me in fifteen minutes. What I want now is something that'll plow through brush. I feel like a fool toting a shotgun in deer woods, but somebody's got to get the meat for this camp. I can see that right now!"

He left us, a sturdy, indignant figure in the old brown mackinaw, buttoned as always only at the throat, its brown checks bedizened with red bandannas. We wear red in the Wisconsin deer woods. Pat and I went into the brush and separated within a mile.

It was one of the grandest hunting days I remember. The kindly old hills took me in. They let me become a part of them. Up this ridge and down that one. Across that draw on the outside near yonder hump. Maybe a buck would come along. Who cares? Still-hunting? Not even that. Just poking about in the hills.

I had been tired, but now seemed refreshed. The previous day I had driven 460 miles over a large part of Wisconsin's deer country. I felt I needed to get out and replace the fatigue of driving and city life with the honest weariness of the woods. I wanted to get out and perspire and breathe hard climbing hills.

That country has an enthralling sweep. It fascinated me as it had fascinated Pat for years. It seems more like a mountain country than anything I know of in Wisconsin. Not in the sense of possessing high ranges; indeed not. But it has contrast, and contrast is what counts. Sometimes a child's sand mounds in the back yard can look more like mountains than the real thing.

A mountain country in miniature. But quite accessible to a man on foot. A place where a man can feel a giant by his conquest of one range after another. A bewildering assortment of crazily strewn sand-hills, the product of the last glacier.

A place where a hunting man can find a thousand spots to stand with a modern arm and command a mile of country. A place where high, wooded ridges run helter-skelter. One of those rare, pockmarked terrains of the lake states where you can actually put field-glasses to good use, where hunting can be made more like bighorn stalking than deer hunting.

It's north of the town of Barnes in Bayfield County, but you've got to get off the town roads and fire lanes to see it. Furthermore, if you're interested in the travelogue angle, have a peek some day at the somewhat less rolling land south of the Eau Claire Lakes in that same county, along what they call the Hayward Road. One opening day of deer season I counted—But hold on; we're off the trail.

Fifty years ago the lumbermen took off the white pine. "The finest white pine that ever grew," they tell. They've been pecking away since at the smaller stuff. Now they're down to jack-pine pulpwood, but an amazingly benevolent nature is building back. Leave it alone and keep the fire out, and it will come back, they who know tell us.

Stand on one of those ridges and look far away. Have you ever tried to look at anything far away in a city? Or even in a town? I mean something that rests the eye. The eye seems to forget it can be made to focus at long distances. Far-off misty blue hills, one draped behind the other; ropy, twisted hills; tree-clad ridges; old pot-holes that once were lakes; long, inviting draws. No part of it like any other part.

Perhaps what Pat and I saw in those hills that day is of small moment. Perhaps here, in an outdoor magazine devoted to fishing, hunting and kindred sports, is no place to confess

hunting was secondary out there in the sun-drenched hills.
Perhaps . . .

But I doubt it. I know too many Pats and Jims and Johns.
I know how they feel some days. I grew up in deer country.
As a boy, it was important that my dad get his two legal deer
that the law allowed. It was meat for the winter. I grew up,
like many another youngster in north Wisconsin, with venison a familiar and delicious taste. From about seven on I
used to be as thrilled as any adult hunter when enough snow
fell at the opening to "make for good trackin'."

But it is something to be alone in the bush with a .30-30
under your arm, the wind in the trees and the feeling that if
there are such things as big cities they must have existed in
some ancient past. It is a fine thing to climb a rise, sit in the
tumbleweeds, smoke a pipe and look off for miles at more of
the same country you just came through.

Some people ask why men go hunting. They must be the
kind of people who seldom get far from highways. What do
they know of the tryst a hunting man keeps with the wind
and the trees and the sky? Hunting? The means are greater
than the end, and every deer hunter knows it.

The yellow November daylight was fading fast when I
turned back toward the parked car. The last half mile took
me over the highest hill I had found. I hadn't seen a deer!
But the sun was molten and round in the west over the upper
Brule country. South, like a straight brown carpet, ran a
wide, new fire lane. Here and there lights on hunters' cars
were already gleaming in the dusk.

At the car I found Pat. He had just arrived. We were both
leg-weary but uplifted. The President had not appeared. The
sun went behind the hills, and the quick November darkness
came on from the east. Pat was reminded that we had played
a rather shabby trick on Mister President. He rubbed his
chin and remarked, "If he gets a critter, we'll never hear the
end of this."

I felt guilty myself. "But, of course," I reminded Pat, "he won't get a deer." The President is a "drive man."

An old car creaked out of the narrow trail down which we had seen the President vanish four hours ago. The driver, a sturdy son of the hills, rolled down a window and shouted: "You fellows looking for an old gent with a shotgun?"

"Not exactly," we explained. "He's back there 'bout half a mile with a 180-pound buck, and he told me to tell you boys he'd be durned if he'd move him an inch from where he dropped him."

"Man with a brown mackinaw draped with bandannas?"

"That's your man. He can't tote that buck out alone."

The messenger of the hills drove off.

Pat spoke first. "Maybe we'd better just go home and go quietly to bed with the covers over our heads."

"I am beginning to get your idea, Dr. Tierney."

"He's had me under suspicion ever since the last day of the duck season," Pat went on. "I wanted to quit at noon because I was cold."

We drove the car down the trail among the scratchy oaks. The President was sitting at the roadside smoking a cigarette. The buck lay in the center of the trail, where he had dropped it. He had dressed it, sat down and waited.

"I told that fellow in the car I wouldn't move him," the President explained. "Told him why, too. Told him I had a couple naturalists with me who liked hard work. He seemed to enjoy it. Anyway, he drove his car through the brush to avoid running over the buck. And how did my—er—er—companions of the chase make out?"

At that, he didn't bear down so hard. He seemed to be waiting for something. He wouldn't touch the buck. No, sir. Not with two, strong, heavily muscled young athletes around. He'd take care of the winter's meat. But the menial tasks? For the women and children, he said.

We stowed that limp, five-point animal in the trunk of my

car, and there was room for the guns. Then, in the last of the daylight, we looked over the place.

It was easy to see what had happened, once the President showed us. The trail was an old logging road. The President had looked it over carefully for a distance of several hundred yards. It lay just on the edge of that wide hill country. He chose the brushiest spot in the road because, going into the woods from the trail on each side, he had found a deer runway, hard-packed in places, with hooked brush where bucks had worked off steam.

Thirty yards from that crossing, almost invisible from the trail itself, the President had sat down to wait. One hour. Two hours. Two and a half. He knew which way the buck would come. From the hills where "you two boys were running up and down the ridges."

A twig snapped. A hundred yards back from the trail, on a rise, came the buck, walking, nibbling a bit here and there. He was obviously working cagily out of the hills toward a game refuge to the west. The President held his fire. He wasn't sure of that first barrel. The buck would stay on his own runway and hit the road. The wind was right. The President doesn't make that kind of mistake. The buck walked leisurely into the open center of the road. He was thirty yards away.

"I decided right then and there to pull the rear trigger!" the President explained. "That buck never knew what hit him. Both slugs at once through the neck. Say, that shotgun's got the old flat-shooter beat at close range."

We made it to the camp, hung the buck on the pole and went inside. It was warm in there. Pat and I removed our heavy flannel mackinaws, and then our flannel shirts. We sat and talked. The President's revenge was not forthcoming. Maybe he had forgotten about it in the elation at getting his buck. He was very kind to us. He made two trips to the kitchen to pump us cold drinks from the big red pump. What with him being so nice, we could hardly refuse when he asked us to carry in an armload of wood apiece for the fireplace.

We returned. The wood clattered to the floor beside the hearth. The light was poor, I noticed. Something was draped over the shade of the big gasoline lamp. I removed it—two pieces of flannel, one green and black, the other red and black. It was, in fact, the major portions of the shirt-tails of Pat Tierney and your reporter. The President had deftly snipped them off when we had gone for the wood. From a corner of the room, where he lay wreathed in tobacco smoke, the President of the Old Duck Hunters peered at us and chortled.

"Now," he said, "you danged naturalists can get me my supper."

With its blend of buffoonery and benevolence,
The Kitchen-Sink Fish *may be MacQuarrie's*
most well-remembered story. The one always
talked about by those who followed the yarns
in the late 1930's and early 1940's.

4

Who can forget Mr. President peering
through the bushes saying, "Fell in on purpose
so I'd feel sorry for you, eh?"—then throwing
his jacket around his pal's shoulders. Calling
the spot where he himself was inadvertently
pulled into the water the "place where I swam
the Brule and later hanged a man on a handy
cedar tree." Filling the coffee thermos with ice
water for the shivering MacQuarrie.

"Mac made people envy him," a fellow
writer said. "It was one of the tricks of his
trade." That's true. You envy the fun he has
with Mr. President. You envy the great appre-
ciation he has for his fishing and hunting.
He makes you like him. Reading the stories,
it is inevitable that you find yourself wishing
you were smoking a pipe, leaning back
against a river, trying to fool a fish. It
was a trick of his trade.

The Kitchen-Sink Fish

In the month of May, when spring is a blessed fact in most places, churlish Lake Superior declines to be a good neighbor. This greatest of fresh-water bodies hangs on to departing winter by its coat-tails, fights hard to keep its vast ice-fields from withering before the prairie winds. Some days the westerly winds drive the ice-floes beyond sight of land. Then the wind shifts, and back come the chalk-white rafts to jam the bays and harbors and river mouths. When the lake wind is king, its cold will be felt some distance inland.

A strange climate, this. Raw winter in control on the lake shore many a day when, fifteen miles inland, the country is soaking up 70- and 80-degree warmth. At least one newspaper in a lake-shore city has acknowledged this whimsical weather by publishing, daily in spring, the temperature not only of the city but of the interior at a point thirty miles away. Thus lake dwellers learn when they may escape the cold wind in a game of golf, a country ride—or a bit of fishing.

Now, coursing down for sixty-six miles to the south shore of this chilly old lake is the river Brule. Early in the season this estimable trout stream may, in its upper reaches, soak in 90 degrees, while down below, near the lake, the Brule runs through temperatures of 45 or 50 degrees.

Strange things can happen to a fisherman in Maytime along this storied Wisconsin stream. A man can fish it of a morning

49

near the lake and see ice form in his rod guides. Later, hunting the sun, he can drive to an upper river put-in and get his neck thoroughly sunburned, and wish to high heaven he had left off the long underwear.

You who fish it—and every troutster hopes he will—should be forewarned so that you may come with clothing appropriate both for late winter and full summer. The only solution is two kinds of apparel. Many's the time I have hit the lower Brule dressed like an Eskimo, and then gone upstream and cooled my feet by dangling them over the side of a canoe.

A good many of the faithful, like the President of the Old Duck Hunters' Association, Inc., are firm believers in celebrating the opening along the more arctic portions of the Brule. There is sound reason for this. At the average opening many of the big, migratory rainbows from Lake Superior have finished spawning and are working back to the home waters.

"A man would be a ninnyhammer," said Mister President to me, "to pass up that first crack at the big ones."

"Habit is a powerful thing," said I.

Well did he know my affection for the upper reaches and its chance for trout, albeit smaller ones, on smaller lures: namely and to wit, dry floating flies, than which no finer device to deceive fish has been conceived in the mind of man.

Anyway, we went fishing on the lower river, come opening day. It was a morning to gladden pneumonia specialists. Emerging from the warm car at the streamside, I was as eager to embrace the flood as I am to get up in a deer camp and light the fire. Braver men than I have quailed at such fishing. I can remember huge Carl Tarsrud, stellar Brule fisherman, six feet four of Viking stamina, declaring in John Ziegler's gun repair shop that he wouldn't have any part of that lower Brule on an ugly first day.

Well, there we were, us Old Duck Hunters, as far asunder in fraternal spirit as ever we were. It made me shiver just to

look at that part of the Brule. We were down below Armstead's farm, north of the town of Brule. There were snowy
patches in the hollows, the day was gray, and from the lake
blew a searching cold.

The Rt. Hon. President was lively as a cricket. His brown
eyes snapped. He had buckled into waders while I was pulling
on extra socks—reluctantly. For him the birds were singing
and the sun was shining. In him the flame of the zealot burns
with a fierce light. He went to the river whistling. I followed
in a dampened frame of mind.

Against the rigors of the day I had seen to it that there was
a full quart thermos of scalding coffee in my jacket. I knew,
too, that the President was similarly fortified, from the bulge
in his own jacket. As I waded out into the rocky stream it
came to me that, if worst came to worst, it was always
possible to go ashore, light a fire, and drown my woes
guzzling coffee.

Hizzoner had no thought of coffee at the moment. He
hastened away down the little path on the left bank and
embraced the current a hundred yards below me. This was
duck soup for him. You knew, watching even at that distance,
no shiver passed through his wiry frame, and you thought,
disgusted, what frightful fanaticism possesses a man who thus
cleaves to his private poison under any conditions.

I remember how cold I got. I remember how my hands got
blue, how I dreaded changing flies or plucking with numb
fingers for lethargic angleworms in the bait can. I remember
how the river cold bit through waders and wool and drove
me, time and again, to perching on stream rocks. I remember
how I thought wader pockets would be handy things to have,
and how I pressed hands into armpits to restore warmth.

But, best of all, I remember the big splash I made when
worn hobnails betrayed me and I bounced, more horizontal
than vertical, off a flat rock into four feet of water. Then
the river claimed me completely, so that my under wools and

my outer wools were soaked and only a wild grab saved my hat from drifting away.

Ah—the coffee! And the warming fire! A big one. And may the devil fly away with every rainbow trout in the lower Brule, for all of me. They weren't hitting anyway. Blessed coffee. Blessed fire.

Now for a match. Whazzat, no match-safe? Had I left it home this evil day, after toting it for years and years? I had, verily. Oh, foolish man. Oh, bitter cold. Well, the coffee, then. And quick, Henri, for there's a man freezing to death! Ah—a whole quart, scalding hot!

I unscrewed the aluminum top and gazed into a container in which the fragile glass shell had broken into a million pieces. Those old, smooth hobs on my wading brogues had not only half drowned me, but had delivered the thermos to mine enemy, the rock.

A pretty pickle. In ten minutes I'd be ready for an oxygen tent. I have fallen into many a river and many a lake. Annually I achieve swan dives, jack-knifes, half-gainers and standing-sitting-standing performances. I am an expert faller-in. Poling a canoe up Big Falls on the Brule, I can, any day you name, describe a neat parabola and come up dripping with only one shin skinned. On my better days I can weave back and forth in exaggerated slow motion until the waters finally claim me.

Be assured, gentlemen, you are listening to no raw beginner at the diving game. But that one down below Armstead's farm really won me the championship of the Brule that season. That one was an even more convincing demonstration than one of several years before, when I fell head first out of a duck boat and went home by the light of the moon, strictly naked, my underwear drying on an oar.

"For two bits," I said, thinking of Mister President, "I would go look him up and give him a taste of it himself." It was just then the trail bushes parted, and there he was, dry

as a bone, grinning like a skunk eating bumblebees, the tail
of a big rainbow projecting from his game pocket. He took
me in at a glance.

"Fell in on purpose so I'd feel sorry for you and we'd go
to the upper river, eh?"

So much for sympathy from this Spartan who, when he
falls in, keeps right on a-going. Nevertheless he produced his
hot coffee and dry matches. While the fire roared and I
draped clothing on bushes, he told me about the fish. "Down
by those old pilings. Salmon eggs. I went downstream with
him forty yards. He was in the air half the time."

Then he noticed that his ghillie was, in fact, in the blue-
lipped stage. He took off his jacket, threw it around me and
pushed me closer to the fire, throwing down birch bark for
me to stand upon. It seemed to me there lurked in his eyes a
twinkle of sympathy, but I can never make sure about that
with him. It may be deviltry. He built a drying frame for the
wet clothes, and when an hour had passed and I was back into
them, half dry and very smoky, he relented completely. He
went the whole hog.

"Well, come on. You'll never get completely dry down
here. I've got my kitchen-sink fish anyway."

The President thus describes the whale which he must
annually stretch out in the sink before calling in the
neighbors.

So it was that we pulled out of the lower Brule valley and
drove south. In the town of Brule he stopped the car and
went into a store with his now empty thermos bottle.

"A man has got to have coffee to fish," he said.

It was only around noon, and this far up the Brule valley
the sun was shining. South we went over familiar trails: the
ranger's road past round-as-a-dime Hooligan Lake, the county
trunk, past Winnebojou where three hundred cars were
parked and thence to Stone's Bridge where Johnny Degerman
presided. Up there it was 75 above. There was a strong, gusty

wind beating downstream. It was summer, and a few minutes before we had been in winter.

Let it be said here that on opening day along the Brule people who like to be alone will do best to stay above Winnebojou. Along this portion of the creek, for some twenty miles, most of the banks are owned privately, and ingress to same is not to be had at every turn-in gate along the county roads that parallel the stream. But the problem can be solved by going to Stone's Bridge, the common jumping-off place for upper river explorers.

If it is feasible to divide any river into two parts, the division may be effected on the Brule by nominating the Winnebojou Bridge as the equator. And connoisseurs of the difference between fact and fancy should be told, right here and now, that people who really know the creek will always refer to this particular spot as the Winnebojou Wagon Bridge, and you can figure out yourself when the last wagon crossed any bridge anywhere.

Still that is its traditional name. Upstream from it lie several million dollars' worth of real estate and lodges, including the fabulous Pierce estate of 4,400 acres. Downstream from it are the precincts of Tom, Dick and Harry and, let it be added, the best places for getting the big rainbows in the early run.

It was so warm up there at Stone's Bridge that Johnny Degerman, Charon of these waters, had his shirt open all the way down the front.

"Mr. Degerman, I believe," said the President in his best manner.

"Go to hell, the both of you," said Mr. Degerman, who was being bothered some by mosquitoes.

"Mr. Degerman!" the President reprimanded.

"I saved a canoe," said Johnny. "Thought you might be along. Could have rented it for five bucks. And all I get from you birds is a buck."

"Mr. Degerman," said the President, "your philanthropy

moves me to the extent of promising to pay one buck and a half for said canoe."

"Lucky if I get the buck," said Johnny, who is a charming fellow. "And say, if you're smart, you'll show them something wet and big and brown. Carl Miller has been knocking their ears off with a big home-made Ginger Quill."

"Enough!" cried Hizzoner. "First you insult me, and then you rub it in by telling me what to throw at 'em. Gimme a canoe pole. I mean give him one. My back ain't so strong today."

So it was that the old Duck Hunters went forth abroad upon the bosom of the Brule and Mr. Degerman called after us, "I may pick up some chubs for you off'n the bridge, in case you don't connect."

We were too far away for the President to do more than look back at Johnny with what must pass as a haughty stare.

It was certainly a day. There was that downstream breeze, which means warmth. There was the smell of a million cedar trees. There was a good canoe under us, and ten miles of red-hot river before us, and hundreds and hundreds of cedar waxwings letting on they were glad to be alive.

You know how it is. The signs are right. You feel history is in the making. You take your time buttering up the line. You are painstaking about soaping the surplus grease off the leader. You lay on the anti-mosquito kalsomine. You light a leisurely pipe and don't give a rap what happens tomorrow or the day after.

His nibs exercised seniority rights by occupying the bow with a rod the first hour. It was not too eventful. Small trout could be had for the casting, willing wallopers, mostly rainbows and brookies, which fought with terrier impudence. The worthier foes were lurking under the banks and in the deep holes. The only memorable excitement in five miles was a dusky native of about 16 inches which came out from under a brush heap to take the President's wet Cowdung.

For long years those upper Brule brookies have intrigued the O.D.H.A., Inc. We do not credit them with too much sense. But accuse us not of sacrilege, for we love them dearly. We love them so much that we wish they had more—well, foresight. In a hitting mood they are fly-rushers, show-offs, and that is the trouble. More common caution and less eagerness to lick the world would save many of them useless flops in the bottom of a willow-walled hereafter.

"Did I ever tell you about the Olson boys?" said the President at lunch at May's Rips. "They were taking out pine on a forty near Foxboro, and it was a whale of a big forty, because they got about a million feet off it one winter.

"Anyway, one morning, the kid—I forget his name—woke up late in the camp and began dressing. He couldn't find his socks, which is what happens to anyone who wakes up late in a well-regulated logging camp. So he says, says he: "Some low-down, no-good miscreant without the decency of a weasel swiped my socks! Was it you, Pa?""

There was more. Of Jack Bradley's aniline-dyed pigeons which he sold to visiting trout fishermen on the Big Balsam in the old days as holy birds of India. Of the same Jack's famous kangaroo court, where fishermen were sentenced for ungraceful lying. Of times along the storied Brule when lumberjacks took out brook trout by the bushel on red-flannel-baited hooks. And there were tales of Old Mountain, the Brule's mythical gargantua, a rainbow trout whose ascent of the stream raised the water two feet; of his sworn enemy, the Mule, another rainbow, almost as big. That sort of thing didn't catch many fish, but along the Brule you are likely to feel it doesn't make any difference, one way or another.

We sat there, with our backs against cool cedars, and watched the river hustle by. Sometimes a canoe drifted past and a lazy hand would be raised, or a lazier Chippewa would exert himself for a minute, poling up the not-too-formidable fast water of May's Rips. But mostly we just sat and studied foam-flecked water spill down the rips, arrow into a water spear-head at the bottom and carom off to the left. It was almost three o'clock when the President leaped up.

"I don't know why in time I go fishing with you," he declared. "The day is almost over, and I've got only one kitchen-sink fish."

"Gimme," said I, "another doughnut—and shut up, will you?"

But the spell was broken. Mister President was on his feet and there was a river to fish. I took the stern paddle, for it was my turn, and the canoe slid down May's Rips, under the rustic bridge, past the Pierce hatchery outflow, through the wide-spread and down threatening Big Falls, which looks worse than it is, but is bad enough.

Big Falls is just a good fast rip of river, almost completely arched by graceful cedars. You see it from the upstream side as hardly more than an inviting dark tunnel in the cedar forest wall. You see a little lip of curling water; and then when you are right on top of it and your eyes are adjusted to its darker light, you see it as a downhill stretch of roaring water, and unless you are good at twisting canoes around right-angled corners you may have trouble at the end, where it goes off to the left.

Big Falls is just another rapid to a good Brule Chippewa boatman. But neither the President nor I qualify in that respect. We are fair, just fair. On good days, when we are not too tired, we can, with care, bring a canoe back up Big Falls, a stunt the Chippewas do with a passenger—usually sitting, tensed, in the bottom. Well, Big Falls has licked me more often than vice versa, but I am resigned to winning up to about the eighth round, after which I fall in, or out, and grab the bow of the canoe and tow it the rest of the way.

We got down easily, and in the slack water the President said: "Hold 'er! Hold 'er and give me my waders."

For once, I had thought, we were to hit the upper river

without recourse to long halts while Mister President climbed in and out of waders. It was not to be so, however. He had his same old scheme in mind: to tie up the canoe and wade the fast water below the Big Falls. He is a man who holds that the best way to catch trout is to meet them on their own terms, afoot.

Below Big Falls the Brule is touch-and-go wading in many spots. It goes down and it twists. It shoots between banks of huge gray cedars, and in places the trees almost meet overhead. Its bottom is rock-strewn. Its current is swift. Here, you would say, is a hunk of river that would be at home in the mountains.

Big fish have come out of that water. Springs seep out of the banks, and watercress flourishes in the sodden places where the river and terra firma contest for control. All of it—river, bank and trees—are forest sponge, and through this rolls gin-white water over knobby bottoms.

I saw Hizzoner get down to business with salmon eggs and spinner. I went at it myself with Degerman's recommended Ginger Quill. Oh, there were fish. There are always frying-pan fish in this stretch. Mostly rainbows, here and there a brown that forgot to wait until night, and some brooks. In such swift water things can be very exciting with nothing more than a foot of fish on a line.

I saw the good fish—the No. 2 kitchen-sink fish—hit. It was Mister President's salmon eggs he coveted. A rainbow tardy in its return from waters so far upstream. But there was nothing tardy about the way it whacked the salmon eggs. These fish conjure up a kind of electrical insanity when they feel cold steel.

Hizzoner gave it the butt and yelled. I climbed out on the bank and went down there to view the quarrel. It was getting on toward evening. The river chill was rising.

Mister President's rod—the one with the long cork grip to

ease the hand—got a workout that day. Above the rapids
he yelled, "For the love of—"

The rest of his conversation was swallowed by river
sounds, for it is so noisy in those rips that you can smile
at a partner, call him a no-good stiff and he will actually
think you are complimenting him. However, I gathered that
the President desired that I make a pass at the big rainbow
with a little metal-rimmed net which I carried. His own
deep-bellied net was back in the canoe.

The fish was a good, standard, spring-run Brule job. Maybe
around five pounds. Six pounds, possibly. My net was no
instrument for him, but that's what I thought Hizzoner had
ordered, and I went to work, all eyes on the fish.

He let him leap, up and down and across. There is no
stopping these fellows when they start. Not for nothing
do they wear that red badge of courage along the lateral
line. When they get tired of plowing the top water, they
just lie like stubborn terriers holding to a kid's skipping rope
and tug-jerk! jerk! jerk!

Mister President was bellowing over the roar of water. I
did not hear him. I was intent on getting that little net
under the fish. The rainbow was brought close. I saw him
a few feet from me—a hard, swift bullet of a fish, ready
for another dash.

My time had come, and I swooped. I swooped with the
net and missed.

Only in nightmares do I recall it clearly. The rim of the
net touched that walloper somewhere, and with one powerful
twist he was off and away, a shadowy torpedo heading for
deep water.

I was a bit downstream from his nibs. I worked back
toward him so that I could hear what he had been shouting.
Coming closer, I heard: "I was telling you all the time to
go back to the canoe and get my net, dern ye!"

That must have unnerved me, for when I got near him a

foot slipped. I reached out for support, got hold of Mister President's shoulder and both of us went down.

To this day the Hon. President refers to that stretch as "the place where I swam the Brule, and later hanged a man on a handy cedar tree."

It was too late for a drying fire. There were miles of upstream poling ahead of us. We had the Big Falls to negotiate the hard way. So we got in the canoe and started. Mister President took the rear; I worked a shorter pole in the bow.

Half-way up, I knew we'd make it. We synchronized well as a poling team. The old knack was there. We would both heave with the poles at just the right instant, and get a fresh hold on the bottom at the right time. For once, said I, the Big Falls would find me triumphant.

Only one of us made it, and it was not I. With about ten feet more to go, the canoe gave a sudden and unaccountable jerk, not caused by rocks, you understand. Once more yours truly was overboard. That one, as I recall, was a quick back dive, and while I floundered, waist deep, Hizzoner shot the canoe up the last curling lip of the rapids.

To this day he will admit nothing. He declares such occurrences are part of the hazards of the game. He avers maybe his pole did slip a bit when it should have remained firm, that maybe he did shift his feet just a trifle. But as for admitting he put me overboard—"You know I wouldn't do a thing like that."

It was getting dark when I caught up with him at the head of Big Falls. He was grinning and had his recently filled thermos bottle open and ready for me. I wrung out such garments as I could and thanked the stars for that warm coffee. I raised it to my lips there in the dusk, and I was chilled to the core.

It contained only ice-water. Ice-water! Of which I had recently drunk enough to float the canoe. From the semi-darkness came his voice: "I thought you'd get so hot up here on the upper river you'd need a cooling drink."

Later, while warming with the upstream poling job, he said that once he saved a man's life. The man had fallen in a lake and was well-nigh a goner. He fished the fellow out, squeezed out the water and restored him to consciousness with a hatful of lake water dashed into his face. The fellow came around, said Mister President, ran his tongue over his lips where the water lingered and said, "Dang it, you know I never tech the stuff!"

So we went home with only one kitchen-sink fish, and I was warm as toast long before we got to Johnny Degerman's dock. Which may have been from exertion with a canoe pole, or may have been from listening to the President of the Old Duck Hunters' Association, Inc

"*It's done me a power of good to see you light into this game over the last ten years and come to love it for its own sake.*" The President is talking at the close of this story. He is seldom this complimentary and MacQuarrie is moved. "*I'm not a sentimental man, as you know,*" he continues, "*but at this time I want to say you measure up . . .*"

5

MacQuarrie is carried away. Barely, he manages to thank the old man for these unexpected words.

"*You measure up in almost every respect.*" The President goes on. "*There is only one more thing for you to prove.*" MacQuarrie is eager, like a little trout rushing for the fly. "*Yes?*"

"*Just how neat you are around the corners in washing storm-windows.*"

It was an odd thing, the way the presence of Mr. President uplifted Gordon MacQuarrie's writing. In his declarative pieces MacQuarrie was another good outdoor writer. He had style and humor; he was knowledgeable and clear. Only when Mr. President entered the stories did the words take on added dimension.

The reason is clear and is stated in Johnny's Pot-Hole for the first time. "*Many times I have watched Mr. President—in duck blinds, on trout streams, in upland bird cover, in deer woods—and have come to believe that the things of the outdoors which he symbolizes are a way of life.*"

In other words, the old man with all his chicanery and wit, his capacity to enjoy, his penetrating honesty, his expertness, has become a symbol. MacQuarrie doesn't know it, but Mr. President is to become the foil through which the author will be able to share with his fellow-man the lessons he learns about the purpose of existence and the meaning of life.

Johnny's Pot-Hole

The Old Duck Hunters' Association, Inc., practically stole Johnny's pot-hole. It wasn't out-and-out claim-jumping. Rather an ethical, legalized pre-emption for which Johnny has only himself to blame. He made the mistake of driving out by his secret road too early one afternoon when the Association was picking up decoys on a near-by, less favored lake.

There was Johnny in his old puddle-jumper with trailer and boat behind and a guilty look on his face. The guilty look was due to the fact that the Old Duck Hunters and Johnny, being old friends, had recently exchanged official information on available wet places in northwest Wisconsin where a fellow would find plenty of last night's duck feathers floating on this morning's water.

The waterfowl pact between Johnny and the Association had been cemented and celebrated with the official purchase by the Old Duck Hunters of a dozen solid black decoys made by Johnny, the same being cunning devices for attracting the sociable bluebill. So you can see why Johnny was red around the ears that dreary wet afternoon when his car wallowed out of a place in the brush where the Association had not dreamed there was room even for a man afoot.

It must be said for Johnny that he repented on the spot. He told all. He walked the Old Duck Hunters back in the scrub a bit and showed them where an agile automobile in the hands of a stump-jumping expert could be driven about a mile to the shore of a little pot-hole lake. The revelation was more than illuminating because ingress and egress in this fashion were of necessity via three hard-hunted lakes where bluebill campaigners are present all season.

Johnny explained that it had become increasingly difficult for him to guard his secret. He had been forced to go to his pot-hole while other hunters lay abed, and he had always gauged his departure to avoid the last of the boys pulling out after shooting ceased. The day we caught him, he had left earlier because he had to be back on his job as a city fireman. And if you ever hear of a single vote against the platoon system for fire-fighters in Superior, Wisconsin, that will be Johnny uttering his dictum against a system that betrayed him.

To this day, Johnny's pot-hole is known to only a few hunters, which is nothing unusual for pot-holes in north Wisconsin. When you have some 5,500 lakes, many of them unnamed, there are bound to be some places that the boys just don't find. The business of concealing these places can be a high art. We once knew a county highway commissioner who issued a road map every year or so. He was an ardent fisherman. And that is why the map, each year, showed fewer and fewer of the old lumbering-day trails giving access to untouched parts of rivers. The commissioner "seen his duty and done it."

In the season of which I write, the O.D.H.A. had been holding lodge meetings regularly in some of the upper state's best duck wallows. The final day was not far off. The last week-end was at hand. I crossed the street to proposition the leading spirit of this two-man fraternity.

"Can't go," he said. "She—the supreme court—says I've got to wash and put on the storm-windows."

As we talked the northwest wind was rising. Sparrows

were chattering under the eaves earlier than usual. I insisted we had to go and that Johnny's pot-hole was the spot. Mention of the place brought reminiscence: "Um. Yeah. Always remember it as being four miles from the creek where Chad and I used to sneak up on the brook trout with telescopic rods. I'll see what she says."

He returned after a brief conference with the head of his household and announced: "I can go. All I had to do was promise her you'd help with the storm-windows. You can wash 'em, and I'll put 'em on. Remember, I did it all for the Association!"

I didn't protest. He is endowed with power of attorney to represent me in all the Association's interests. The well-known Senegambian in the woodpile is bound to appear under such an arrangement, but it's worth it.

The rite of breakfast was under way in the presidential manor early next morning when I appeared. Which means when the President presides, a breakfast of everything from flannel cakes to three cups of he-man coffee. We loaded the car and departed.

The wind was stronger. The signs were good. South we drove for sixty miles on a smooth, hard road, our speed limited only by the rut-spraddling machine the President had chosen for this quest.

Off the hard road and east we went, then south again into the heart of the north Wisconsin barren lands. The turn-off at night on the unmarked sand trail is hardly more than an instinctive whirl of the wheel. You come to a familiar hump in the road and turn. That's about all. The barrens are like that.

Through the windshield the unsteady lights became blurred with rain. One of those dawn-beginning rains that at that season in the north is almost certain to turn into snow. The trail was two hard ruts where wheels had cut through turf. The world of the barrens was a soggy black void.

We poked slowly over the trail. Three times we stopped at as many fair-sized lakes and found an inch of ice in all of them. The President was jubilant. One of the requisites for good shooting on Johnny's pot-hole is ice in these three neighboring lakes.

Around the hard-packed beach of the largest of the three lakes we drove. You just don't take a new automobile into such places. Once we drove over and through the remnants of a blind we had built a year before. Then ahead of us lay the almost indiscernible mouth of the road into Johnny's pot-hole.

More good news—Johnny's pot-hole was open. We saw the sullen gray of its water as the jalopy burst through the final fringe of scrub-oak and stopped at the top of a wide sandy beach.

Johnny's pot-hole is deep for its hundred acres or so. It is one of those deep-set, spring-fed pot-holes fairly common in Wisconsin. Not worth much as duck water when other lakes are open, but an almost sure-fire bet late in the season because it is one of the last to freeze.

The President busied himself with the blind. He covered the familiar brown mackinaw with a raincoat and bent to his task. That is one job he insists on doing. He will let you cut the brush, but in the actual fashioning of the blind he does not tolerate bungling assistance. He weaves blinds! And when he is through, there is a hide you can see out of from any side but which ducks seem not able to see through.

There was no dawn. There was, however, a clammy, blowy beginning to daylight in which the whole sky gradually and reluctantly became visible. The tiny pot-hole was white-capped in the center. I pulled on trout waders and walked as far as possible into the steeply shelving bottom to set decoys—Johnny's good black decoys.

The rain fell harder. It came at more of a slant. The wind was freshening from the northwest—"snow by noon," Mister

President predicted. The President retreated, turtle-like, into the collar of the old brown mackinaw which projected over the shoulders of his raincoat. He lit his little crooked pipe. He was a patriarchal figure there in the storm. He said if he were a duck he'd get right out of that country on the night train.

When Mister President gets into any duck blind, he becomes a submarine telescope. His neck twists, almost revolves, it seems with monotonous regularity, like a lighthouse beam at night. All the time he converses, which is most of the time, his searching brown eyes are eager for the far-off movement in thin air that spells ducks. He is especially good at catching them at their game of topping a far bank of trees and sliding down with the dark background to hide their arrival.

The turning neck paused. The brown eyes puckered to slits. The President slowly withdrew into the blind and arranged himself for quick movement. He spread out his right hand to signal "five." I caught a glimpse of them through the lattice work of leaves, low, laboring into the wind toward the decoys. The President signaled with an expressive wave of his hand for me to take those on the right.

They were easy, coming in a-spraddle—chunky, late-flight rascals that we call "northern bluebills" in Wisconsin. Their legs hitched and bucked as supplementary brakes for short, powerful wings.

They were too easy for me. I picked off my No. 1, but my second barrel was too slow. The birds were on top of us, charging the blind, it seemed. Mister President did better. He usually does. He picked the first undismayed bird deliberately, took another in his stride, then stood and swung around to clip a third which landed with a thump on the rain-soaked beach. The old automatic was as good as ever!

I retrieved the bird that had fallen on land. The others would be duly collected at the end of the shoot, when the wind had drifted them to the far shore. In case of aquatic

growth interfering with their drifting inshore we use a casting
rod with a heavy surface plug.

The wind grew sharper, colder. Before noon flat, sticky
flakes of white heralded the approach of Mister President's
predicted snow. That was better. It made the shooting wilder,
harder.

Have you sat thus on a snowy day and squinted through
the white curtain at those mail-carrying bluebills? Have you
had them come at you out of the smother, skirt the edges of
your decoys and vanish into the storm? Have you seen these
birds of passage drop from nowhere, all sails, set, and come
to rest with a "swi-i-ish" right among the decoys? Birds of
passage indeed, but regal birds.

Until you have courted the bluebills in the snow, you have
not tasted of the purer delights of waterfowling. Fat mallards
over a sunny marsh are fine. Planing, twisting teal in early-
season days are sporty. There is pleasure of many sorts in
the harvest of autumn over the ducking grounds; but the
Old Duck Hunters are extremely partial to the bitter last
days, those stormy days when the wild, free things of duck
shooting are abroad in the very wind with the storm.

From time to time the Association would desert the blind
and repair to the puddle-jumper, one at a time, where a thing
called a hot-air heater would operate if you ran the motor.
The danger of asphyxiation was imminent.

Once, while the President was warming his toes and fingers,
I knocked down two birds that had come in suddenly. Merely
glimpsing them in the poor light, more intent on their flight
than their variety, I shouted to the President that I thought
they might be redheads. He opened the door of the puddle-
jumper and howled back at me through the storm, "If they
ain't bluebills, I owe you a box of shells!"

"Taken!"

Later, at the pick-up, I discovered I owed him a box of
shells.

The day wore on, with long pauses between shots. Two late mallards drifted in from nowhere, and the old master raised up and collected the pair of them, taking the drake first, as a gentleman should. The snow piled deeper on the collar of the old brown mackinaw, matching the near white of Mister President's hair. He resurrected a worn army blanket and an old stable lantern from the car, placed a lighted lantern between his knees and spread the blanket over them. Thus, down through the ages, the duck hunters have fortified themselves against the elements. Many times I have thus watched Mister President—in duck blinds, on trout streams, in upland-bird cover, in deer woods—and have come to believe that the things of the outdoors which he symbolizes are a way of life.

At the pick-up I walked around with the wind to the opposite shore and collected the day's bag. It was not a heavy one, but hunting men know the gratefulness with which one gathers the birds at the end of the day. There, on the lonely shore of that storm-beaten little pot-hole lake, I was thankful indeed for such a splendid day. Then is the time when all of us Old Duck Hunters turn our faces to the blast and, though we may look forward to home and a warm fire, feel a great surge of thanks for such days in the open.

It was quite dark when I tied the string about the neck of the decoy sack. By then there was six inches of snow on the ground. We had not thought of it much while hunting. But there might be difficulty in getting out.

Put it down here and now that those trips are best when the road home is something of a problem. I have driven for two hours to cover thirty miles of snow-covered road in duck season. I once drove 240 miles over ice-glazed highways in the preposterous time of fourteen hours. An eternity, it seemed. But it was worth it. The stormy road home is the best road home for the man who would bring back ducks.

The President supervised the final rituals. He plumped the

snowy decoy sack in the back of the car along with the other gear and steered me out of the little tree clump on the edge of Johnny's pot-hole where we had parked. The lights made sparkling tunnels through the tangle as we lurched back over the trail, around the shore of the larger lake and finally reached the wider road. The heater hissed in the floor of the car. The President rummaged for tobacco and pipe, and settled back as we straightened out for home.

"Well, sir," he said, "I want you to know I've seen a lot of duck hunters start from the bottom and work up, but I never saw one take to the game like you."

I was surprised and flattered. Could it be, I wondered, that my years of laboring as handy-man for Mister President were to bear fruit after all? Younger men in the outdoor game value the praise of old-timers above everything. And all of us know there is little enough of it. The President was mellow as he went on.

"You're willing, strong and young," he said. "I wish I could say the same for myself. It's done me a power of good to see you light into this game over the last ten years and really come to love it for its own sake. I'm not a sentimental man, as you know, but at this time I want to say you measure up—"

I managed to thank him in a stumbling fashion.

"You measure up in almost every respect," he continued. "There is only one thing more for you to prove."

"Yes?"

"Just how neat you are around the corners in washing storm-windows," said the President of the Old Duck Hunters.

"Somehow that river seems awful important today, whether there's a fish in it or not." The President is weary in mind and spirit. He wants to get back to the river. He fishes and feels better.

6

Thus is presented another of the great MacQuarrie themes. Alone of any experience, far better than any experience, the outdoors can restore a man's soul. Again and again it runs through his writing.

Can a bowling match restore a man's soul? Watching a basketball game? Or driving a car at high speed? MacQuarrie would be the first to say maybe. Dogma was no part of this man. His answers are all in the form of questions. Or jokes.

But things of civilization wouldn't restore his soul. And the great public conservation movement at present . . . which he did so much to further during the dark days . . . suggests that it does take a mountain or a river or a forest and the ways of the wild to stir men deeply, to enable them to re-establish values temporarily out of joint, and divide the false from the true.

Just the River

"Look here, boy!" It was the voice of the peerless leader of the Old Duck Hunters' Association, Inc. "I am fed up," he pronounced. "Up to here! Get your fishin' tackle, such as it is, and meet me in half an hour by yonder blooming lilac bush."

With that he dropped the daily newspaper neatly on his right toe and booted it some distance, a mighty good boot on a newspaper. I have seen Automatic Jack Manders do worse with a full-grown football.

The mood had been creeping upon Mister President. It was a mood for the times, a disturbance of the spirit—most unusual for Hizzoner. In the first stages of the mood he had cussed the government. Then he felt ashamed and quit cussing the government, and took it out on his neighbors. He complained that Norm wasn't cutting his share of the lawn where their respective grasses overlapped. Finally he went after the help in his business. All five of them sought solace in sly cribbage games at Henry's.

One confessed to me: "The Old Man is a so-and-so. I'd quit tomorrow if I didn't figger he was my own particular so-and-so."

Thus, in some degree, is explained my headlong evacuation of the premises of the leader of the O.D.H.A., Inc. The above explains, too, why I almost slipped in making the sharp turn around the lilac bush. It explains why my wife

73

warned me as I grabbed up scattered gear: "Pick up your feet, buddy, before you break a leg."

And it explains why I was back there at the Old Man's domicile in fifteen minutes, flapping with waders, rod case, jacket and those other essential oddments which release the pent-up soul of man.

He was ready. The oldest car in his garage had been backed out on the driveway. He was tossing armfuls of stuff into it. He was still upset—the perfect picture of a man getting away from it all.

He fairly leaped behind the wheel. His cigar was almost cut in twain a good inch up from the butt. Such a sacrifice of good burning tobacco the President allows only in moments of profound stress.

Despite bald-headed tires, he backed the car savagely down the approach, cut the wheels this way and that, barely halted at the highway and leveled out through the suburbs.

A traffic cop rolled up alongside, took one thoughtful look and shouted before zooming away, "Hey, Al, don't go makin' trouble for me!"

Going just as fast, we passed the cop ten blocks later. Mister President glared at him, and then snorted at me: "He's got a rod of mine, and I gave him the directions for getting into the lower Shee Hoss Creek. He should arrest me?"

Such a fierce mood is, indeed, rare in the President of the Old Duck Hunters. It was respected and deferred to by me, the least important half of this fraternity, but it was not quite understandable. He cleared it up.

"I am sore besieged. I have been through a lot, but nothing ever got me down like this. Maybe I'm getting old. Maybe I'm not old enough."

His business had taken some teriffic jolts. And he was getting on up there. He is old, I thought. Or is he? I wondered and, wondering, breathed a fervent hope that I might grow old like him. I studied him as he drove.

There was a sharp bit of color in his high cheek-bones that noon. The unlit cigar was vanishing, half an inch at a grab. He was tense over the thick, clumsy old steering wheel.

We sped along at a good, round fifty, which was stepping it up for the old crate. We went south and east from the western end of Lake Superior into country where lusty second-growth is trying to make the old-timers forget the virgin pine that once grew there in Wisconsin. The destination was almost automatic.

He spun the wheel sharp left and roaded those poor old tires over some awful gravel. Then he spun 'er sharp right, power-diving down two Lake Superior hills and zooming up the other sides.

At the place where the hundred-year-old spruce stands guard in the field I got out to open the taut barbed-wire gate. Then we drove under the thick-branched spruce. The needles brushed the car top. The Old Man took a deep breath, climbed out the driver's side and walked toward the bank of the Brule River. With each step he was more relaxed.

The Brule comes slicking down for sixty miles to the turn where the big spruce stands. Sixty hard-fought miles where the river has dug its channel through sand, rock, ledge and clay.

The Old Man studied the familiar pattern of current and backwater. When he returned to the car, there was a new peace within him. His lips were bent up in a quizzical grin. He lit the demolished cigar and went so far as to say it was "a pretty day."

"Boy," he said, "which way you want to go?"

"Up," I said, for I knew he liked it down-river.

"All right," he said, and then, when I aimed to help him pull on waders, he snapped, "Boy, get out of here before I kick you a full twenty-five feet into MacNeil's Pool!"

I should have known better than to be over-solicitous. In the years that the Old Duck Hunters have convened there

have been few soft speeches. It is better that way. There have
been tough days through all the seasons in the most brutal
climate of these United States. There have been tiring drives,
bitter battles with duck-blind ice, and down-right dangerous
bouts with sudden winds strong enough to twist an oar blade
from a man's hand.

There have been freezing vigils in the cut-over where the
whitetails roam. There have been back-breaking jobs of poling a canoe upstream. There have been cold arisings in the
dark and sudden colder immersions in sundry waters.

But few soft words. The likes of Mister President will
throttle a soft word with a red bandanna handkerchief and
use in its place a rough word—which is often far and away
the better, the more civilized expression.

We were in a fine place to fish for trout. A score of places
on the lower Brule are justly famed. A man can have his
choice of a steep bank to go down or a river-bottom flat,
such as Mister President had turned into.

It was late August. There might be some early fall browns
from Lake Superior nosing up through those lower waters
on the way to spawning beds away upstream. There might
even be an odd big rainbow or steelhead loafing in a hole. A
goodly number of these run up the Brule in autumn, whether
to spawn or no has not yet been determined. But run they
do, albeit most of the rainbows make their spawning run in
the spring.

"I don't feel up to bucking the current today," Mister
President explained. "I'm just going downstream with some
big bucktails and stuff. I may get quite a piece off by dark.
You got a flashlight?"

I gave him my flashlight. It would be tough stumbling back
along the tangled woods path in the dark. I knew him well
enough to be sure he would stick until long after the whippoorwills began.

"Today," he said, "I may not catch a fish. No, sir. I may

just get out in that there river and go along with it. It's the
river I've been thinking about all the way down here—not
the fish. Never thought I'd ever get into such a frame of
mind. Somehow that river seems awful important today,
whether there's a fish in it or not."

He put in from a sandy flat by the big spruce. The current
reared against his thighs, and he became a part of it. Trout
fishing slows the headlong thinker. Watch one step into a
strong river. He either becomes a part of it, or is bowled
over.

I knelt by the spruce, rigging up. Once in the stream, he
quite forgot me. His rod arm came back, then forward. When
he had worked down to the bend, I saw him miss a fish. He
didn't seem to mind. He kept slogging along in the studied,
measured pace of the experienced wader. Then he disappeared around the bend without so much as a backward
glance.

Time was when I became so absorbed in my own fishing
that I went around bothering people telling them just how
I set a No. 14 dry Hare's Ear (not a No. 12—goodness, no!)
in just the right riffle. Not the riffle at the right bank; the one
at the left bank. I used to go around spouting that sort of
thing; and while that sort of thing is all right, it occupies
little space in the minutes of the Old Duck Hunters'
Association.

Let the technical experts have their own good way. Indeed,
their counsel is sorely needed in many quarters. They speak
good words and do a power of good to the beginners. The
thing is that in this recital the technicalities were of small
moment.

I went beyond the upstream turn, taking the bank path to
a fairly fast, well-aerated stretch. This is a long rip of water.
It is one of the last of the big rapids before the Brule slows
down, loafs over its shifting sand-bars and joins Gitche
Gumee.

I like this water. It is swift, but not too swift. It is dry-fly water. It is nice wading. The surface is broken almost everywhere. I worked out my standard exploratory load, a No. 10 brown bivisible. The omnipresent little rainbows smacked it, but that was all. There were a few tentative flashes underwater which might have been good fish, or might have been my imagination, which goes quite beyond control once I am bucking the Bois Brule.

So I changed, running the gamut from big Ginger Quills to nondescript patterns such as I have collected without number from friendly people who stop me when I pass. It is because I always stop that my fly boxes are so full some days and so empty at other times.

On this day my friendliness paid dividends via a henna-colored proposition of good stiff hackle, a palmer-tied floater that traveled with its chin up. The first fish to try this unnamed treasure was a good Lake Superior brown. He showed me about 18 inches of fish, ran back of me into swifter water, called upon the Brule's current for help and jerked loose.

I'd have liked that fellow. He was thick through the middle and would have bolstered my position in life with Mister President. As it turned out, he made a fool of me by running below me. And I was over-anxious. He did surrender up the matted henna fly.

With a handkerchief, lots of blowing and two drops of oil, I put the thing back into shape and tried it some more. The fly was hot. In ten minutes I had two healthy keepers in the grass-lined back of my jacket, and in another five minutes I had a minor evening trophy, a brown of 16 inches.

I was going great guns. The henna fly was taking a beating, but I worked over it manfully after each fish. I began to hope for that man-sized rainbow, some doughty dish-bellied creature from a dark hole, one which grabs what it wants, then runs stark, staring mad all over the river.

It was not to be so. No big 'un came. No big steelhead

or crimson-streaked rainbow lit into the henna creation. But I was of no mind to complain. The browns were putting on a splendid show.

These late-August browns which come from the big lake are not so choosy as their kin which stay in the stream the season through. The day was fairly bright. I was no more expert than usual. It was just that those newly arrived browns were willing.

Some of them came for it at long range. I'd see them lighting into it from behind a rock, or darting out to take a quick look from some foamy stretch. The ones from the troubled water in midstream were not at all hard to nail. The curtain of rapid water over them was my ally.

And finally I met a sunset that was all too premature. One minute the old haymaker was just about over the tops of the bank cedars; the next it was being swallowed by a tall, distant hill. Time to quit. I climbed out, taking the woods path. Back in the car, I discovered I was weary. I put on dry socks, took another gloating look at the day's dividend and fell asleep in the rear seat.

The Old Man's grunting as he tugged at waders awakened me. I sprang up, groping for a coffee thermos in the heaped car. He was grateful as all-get-out. He who had not eaten happily for a week devoured four sandwiches, three cups of coffee, two bananas and almost half a chocolate cake.

The familiar, happy gleam was back in his eyes. He was tired as anything. He'd lost the flashlight coming back upstream. He'd sprung a leak in his waders. He'd worn himself ragged working down that rocky river; but he was a whole man again.

It was my job to drive home. I backed out of the pasture of the big spruce, not forgetting to replace the taut barbed-wire gate. I drove over the steep, crooked hills and went carefully through the dry rutted-clay road to the solid-surfaced main road. I turned to the dozing leader of the Old Duck Hunters.

"Well, I knocked 'em for a loop, mister."

"Eh?" He came to with a start.

"I say I got a limit of nice browns."

"The hell you say." He was nodding again.

"Got one that'll go a pound and a half."

"Fine, fine! I just went fishing. I just went. . . ." He was barely awake.

"A-hem. Did you—well, did you catch a fish?"

His chin was on his chest, his eyes quite closed as he replied. "Stop at the house and leave me half of yours."

*Yes, there is a quality to the outdoors that
makes it different from bowling or watching
television. MacQuarrie squarely lays it on the
line in this story. It is simply that if you aren't
careful, the outdoors will kill you. It is dangerous. Naked, undisguised death lies always
waiting to discipline the unlearned or
the unlucky.*

7

*Men sufficiently expert to gain membership
in the ODHA, Inc. seldom find it a threat.
Long experience has taught them what can and
can't be done, and their resources are infinite.
Once in trouble, they know how to get out
of it. These two are the last you'd expect
to drown or shoot themselves, or get lost
and panic.*

*So it is significant that MacQuarrie should
abandon his pranks and rejoinders and set
Mr. President—of all people—fighting for his
life against a storm.*

*If there is a reason, MacQuarrie never states
it. But mustn't it be that he finds something
stimulating in this danger equation? That
he feels there is something here certain
men need?*

*Is MacQuarrie trying to say that because a
man can so easily die—and must die—is the
greatest reason to cling tenaciously to life and
make every minute of it count? You're
damn right he is.*

The Day I Burned the Oatmeal

Looking out the office window, I knew that the President of the Old Duck Hunters' Association, Inc., would be phoning soon. A northwest wind was tearing smoke from city chimneys. Pedestrians on the street below leaned into the blast. Lights gleamed from office windows, though it was only 10 A. M. Tracer-bullet snowflakes stabbed at the huddled city.

It was mid-November. The leader of the Old Duck Hunters was right on time with his phone call.

"I'm tied up until noon or after," he said. "I'll meet you at the red cabin some time in the afternoon. If I don't show up, don't wait. Get out there yourself. There'll be ducks moving today."

"But I'd rather wait and go with you."

"Maybe I can make it. But you get out there while this wind is at its peak."

Those were marching orders.

Within an hour I had stowed my gear, including Mister President's favorite emergency ration, which is steel-cut oatmeal. With Jerry, the springer, beside me, I drove the seventy miles to the big red cabin on the hill, around which spread a maze of ducking waters. By the time Jerry and I had turned off the main road the snow was coming in sheets.

Jerry, a faithful 45-pound lump of old-fashioned dog, was

restless in the storm. His nose-prints were all over the car windows by the time I climbed the last sandy hill to the big red cabin. I made things ready indoors while Jerry investigated one of the grandest November storms I ever saw.

I swept out the cabin. It hardly needed it; but the Old Duck Hunters make a fetish of keeping things shipshape, in a blind or in a kitchen. The red cabin is one of our put-ins, the summer home of a friend who, after Labor Day, turns the key over to the Old Duck Hunters, in exchange for which he gets an occasional brace of mallards.

I trimmed the wicks of the kerosene lamps and polished their chimneys. Then I built a fire in the red brick fireplace for its companionship. I spread the thick blankets on the two beds, set the kitchen table and kindled the kitchen range to get that oatmeal started. It takes, says Mister President, just three hours of slow steaming to make steel-cut oatmeal as acceptable to a man as to a horse.

In the growing storm I split chunks of lightning-struck Norway pine. Storm-tossed chickadees came to seek out grubs turned up by the ax in the protected space of the wood-yard. Another good sign. When the chickadees come right to the chopping block for food, there is weather afoot.

Jerry came snuffing back to the wood-yard, his back and muzzle caked with snow. He sat safely away from the flying firewood, obviously disgusted with a man who would split wood on such a promising day. Had not he, Jerry, been abroad and seen wondrous things? He followed me in with the last armload of wood. When I slid the worn double-barrel out of its case, he raced for the door. His strong stubby tail wagged into my legs as I leaned over him to turn the knob and face the storm.

By then it was two o'clock. It seemed later, it was so dark. Jerry and I went down the hill to the shore of Deep Lake, a putting-out place for many far-flung duck points. I was hopeful that Mister President would be here. Sometimes he did not bother to drive his car up the cabin hill, but just parked it in the firm sand at the edge of the lake and set out from there.

I was disappointed at not finding him. Jerry kept waltzing about to emphasize the dire need to go hunting—"For heaven's sake, man, what are we waiting for?" But wait I must. A day such as this, after weeks of bluebird weather, was best shared with someone.

The Deep Bay was roaring, although it is partly sheltered. Boats would take a merciless pounding out there, once they got away from the high bank. Ducks whipped over Jerry and me. In the smother I could not make them out clearly, but knew from their short wing-beats that they were deep divers. It was a fine moment, just standing there, but I wished Mister President's car would come lurching down the road toward the beach.

By 2:15 I decided to carry out the marching orders—"Get out there yourself." Jerry was in the boat as I slid it off the sand into pounding waters. He crept to the prow as I started rowing.

I shall not soon forget the wind that cuffed us as we left the shore. The boat—a tough, flat-bottomed job of steel—was seized and tossed by the hungry wind. Even Jerry couldn't take it with his muzzle over the gunwale. He dropped into the bottom of the boat.

My aim was to cross a partly sheltered portion of Deep Lake to a narrows. Once through the narrows, the idea was to push across Shallow Bay, straight into the face of the wind, to a favorite blind which should be ideal with the wind where it was. I am a handy man with the oars, but one glance at Shallow Bay, beyond the narrows' mouth, changed my mind.

Shallow Bay, five feet at the deepest, was a caldron. Moving water had dug so deeply that the usually clear waters were turgid with gray-green bottom muck, and even aquatic plants, torn from the bottom, were being carried off in the waves.

What to do? If Mister President had been there, two pairs of oars could have been manned and we could have fought across Shallow Bay by sheer force. It was no job for one man. Not that half mile of inland lake, transformed into something approximating a stormy ocean.

Well, I knew a place where a fellow could get in a little shooting without having to take another turn at the oars. This particular country has that in its favor. In season, whatever the weather, a man can manage to get some place where chances will be at least fair.

The spot I had in mind was a half mile down the shore from the narrows to another leg of this sprawling lake, where a point thrust out into fairly deep water. There had been no let-up in the storm; so there was only one thing to do: leave the steel boat dragged up at the narrows, don't even bother with the decoys, and hike to that point. With a pocketful of shells I set out.

The wind was crying fury on the point. This point sticks about fifty yards beyond shore growths. Between the last of the trees and the roaring water the only cover was a tiny blind, built there some weeks before. The wind had knocked it into a cocked hat. With jack-pine boughs I built it up a little. The wind was so strong that when a chunk of blind tore away it slapped me across the neck.

While I fussed with the blind, ducks were riding the gale overhead, coming mostly from the northwest and smashing across the point like dive-bombers. Jerry shivered with eagerness at my feet as I got into the partly rebuilt blind. No decoys. Visibility was about seventy yards—sometimes more, sometimes less. The snow was deep enough now to be measured in inches.

Nail 'em, if you can, when they cross. If you see 'em at all. . . .

I peered through the barrels to make sure they were free of snow. I was ready for a band of bluebills that came at me. They were in and gone so quickly that I got in only the open barrel, and at the report a single fell in a wide slant on the wind-torn waters off the point. Jerry, no non-slip retriever, just a fellow for tearing in, was after it like a shot.

The wind bounced the duck along at a furious pace, but Jerry had marked it well. Half the time he was out of sight, and it was a relief when I made out his round head thrust out in the final act of grabbing and then saw him turn and fight back to shore. He landed some distance down the beach and presented me with a drake bluebill that likely had dined the evening before on some northern Minnesota lake.

That single gave me pause. If I winged one and it dropped out too far, the dog, with a heart too big for his strength, might paddle out there and never come back. After that I was careful to watch the ducks that came from the windward side of the point and nail them as quickly as possible so that they dropped on land or close to it, thus keeping Jerry from risking his precious neck.

Many a shot is passed up under such restrictions, but that was all right. Tomorrow morning the Association would get out together. The wind might be down then. Certainly the ducks would be around. Jerry had some easy pick-ups. I think he was grateful.

It would have been a nice, stormy afternoon if Mister President had been along. If he had been on time, we could have made it across to Shallow Bay point, a great favorite with both of us in a northwest wind. Over there, I thought, we could have picked them just as carefully, only more birds would be moving around. That is the way it had always been. Had he just come on time, then we might have lit a little afternoon fire in back of the Shallow Bay blind—one getting warm, the other watching the end of the point.

If he had just been on time. . . . Men who hunt ducks know

what it means to have that indispensable team-mate on hand when things get too much for one man.

I quit at four o'clock by the wrist watch, a very damp watch, strapped to a damp, chapped wrist. Jerry was hardly more than an animated floor mop, but a happy lad, sniffing and snuffing at my game pocket.

As I hiked back to the narrows it came to me suddenly that one of the other rowboats was gone. If the President had come late he might have taken one and set out alone. I searched for tracks, but could find none. Snow had covered everything. I never could keep track of how many boats that landing beach sheltered; so couldn't even guess if he were out in one.

Just one thing to do—get up that hill and see if he were there in the cabin. God, I hoped he was there, sitting before the fire in the gray sweater vest. Moments like those come back with frightful vividness.

In the warm kitchen the oatmeal was bubbling. The broom stood in its appointed corner. The ticking alarm clock mocked me from its shelf.

I burst through the swinging door into the living room. It was empty! No one had been there. The fireplace screen was untouched. A stick of Norway pine braced it against the face of the opening, just as I had left it. He was out there on Shallow Bay!

I tore out of there and back down the steep path. Jerry was for coming, but I slammed the door on him. It was all plain now. The Old Man had grabbed a boat and then started off alone across that treacherous, screaming Shallow Bay.

What a sap I had been not to wait for him! I should have realized he would try it. Should have realized that was right where he would go in a northwest blow. Should have remembered what he had always said—"Show me the sea on an inland lake I can't ride out in a good rowboat!"

Down the path I went. I tossed off the heavy hunting

jacket. I hit that steel boat a-running and was out in it, rowing.

Away from shore, the wind caught me again. It seemed worse than on my earlier trip. Or perhaps my arms were just weary. I hadn't the faintest idea what I would do if I didn't find him. Maybe he had made the point across Shallow Bay. He could handle a boat—indeed he could. There was comfort in that. Maybe he had landed there and was afraid to try going back in the quartering wind. Maybe . . .

I halted at the narrows. I was heaving like a bellows. There was just one thing to do—catch my breath and get right across to that Shallow Bay blind before it got too dark. The direction didn't worry me so much as the rough water. I could make it across if my rowing arms held out. My heart was hammering.

Then he appeared, and I yelled with relief, a yell that he could not hear in the wind. There he was, rowing for the mouth of the narrows against the wind! He had taken off the old brown mackinaw. His white police suspenders stood out like an X in the fading light, for, of course, his back was to me.

Never in my life has the slivery gunwale of a rowboat felt better in my hands. I found myself over my boots as I hauled him in the last twenty-five feet. His mackinaw floated in the half-filled boat. He picked it up and shook the water out of it. The first thing he said was: "Don't ever mention it to my wife! She'd never let me hunt again."

Then he slapped my shoulder, and between us we hoisted his boat upside down on the sand to empty it—the old ritual of the Association. Ten canvasbacks rolled out of it, and he explained, "I just picked the ones with the longest necks when they came by."

Two pairs of oars whisked us back down Deep Bay and we hurried to the warm cabin. Once inside, I knew that he was trying to hide a great weariness, trying to make light of a bad time. I strung the ducks on the back porch. The wind was rising, if anything, but morning and more of it had little appeal right then.

I poked jack-pine kindling under the kettle where the oatmeal bubbled. Then I swept the hearth, for something to do. Over a bowl of that steel-cut oatmeal he told me what it had been like.

"Halfway over I was sorry I'd started. But there I was, and I made it. I'll bet a thousand ducks passed over that point—in range. Seemed like every web-foot in north Wisconsin was up and moving.

"They'd come busting out of the snow, and I'd let 'em have it. Everything was moving—mallards, redheads, cans, bluebills. Then I picked up and started back."

I helped him pull off his boots and found dry things for him. I brought one of the big blankets and tucked it around his shoulders. He leaned back in his chair before the fire. The warmth from it began to get in its work. The tenseness left both of us, and Jerry's stub of a tail showed he had caught the change in our moods.

I got him a bowl of that precious oatmeal, and he was grinning at me when I handed it to him. I was afraid to say anything. Sentiment of the surface kind is foreign to the Old Duck Hunters. I jiggled the stove lids, piling in more wood. There was supper to get.

And then he yelled like his old self from the other room: "Say, how many ducks did you fetch in?"

"Five, I think."

"H-m-m-m. Ought to be ten. Say, got another dab of that porridge?"

All was well in the big red cabin when I brought the porridge, for he said: "Tomorrow morning we'll go back across Shallow Bay, wind or no wind." Then he added: "Damn it, you burned the oatmeal!"

*Why are we not all like Mr. President? Why
do we not all endow inanimate things with
life . . . then make friends with them? Min
and Bill; two wooden duck decoys. Bill with
a fissure down his back you can stick your
finger in. Both a hundred years old and
game to the core.*

8

*No shirking by these hoary two. No
demanding higher wages or complaining that
working conditions be improved. Come what
may, count on them out in the decoys doing
their level best to attract ducks for Mr.
President. Trusted companions of the chase.
Old pals. Game to the core.*

*Childish! Ridiculous! Like a little boy and his
Teddy Bear. No one would agree quicker
than Hizzoner. MacQuarrie has already said he
will never lose the quality of youth and so
grow old.*

*And isn't it better? More fun? Isn't it a
glorious love of life that puts an affectionate
arm around old Min and Bill? Why don't
you start cultivating fun, creating pleasure,
wherever you go, whatever you do?*

Like Mr. President.

Set a Thief . . .

It was precisely the night for the Old Duck Hunters' Association to be about. The October dusk had been snuffed out by a cold rain. Beneath streetcorner lights the last of the brown leaves gleamed wet and sad.

The house of the President of the Old Duck Hunters loomed ahead. I sloshed through the downpour toward the driveway at the back door, knowing that one or another of his faithful second-hand vehicles would be there, patiently accepting hunting gear, though its rear springs sagged to the hubs.

A neighbor's dog, shunted out for his final airing, snarled at me as I went along, and then wagged an apology after a sniff of recognition. I went on, and the dog returned to his front porch.

The light from Mister President's back porch hardly lit the space ten feet away. The patient old car was there, droopy toward the rear like an overworked laying hen. I tossed my stuff into the broad space between back seat and back of the front seat. There was a thermos bottle on Mister President's stoop, and I put that in too. I might then have gone in to pay respects to Mrs. President, but my slicker dripped and I knew she had just polished the floors. So I waited for Hizzoner.

I expected he would issue from the back door with a final armful. Usually it was like that. I would be ahead of him and waiting, and he would come out vowing that I was a half-hour ahead of time, which I usually am.

I got behind the wheel of the car in the semi-darkness and waited. A sound from the back yard of Mister President's next neighbor caught my attention. It was a sound like a man with a burden bumping his knees into a concrete bird bath. Rolling down the window, I confirmed that when Mister President growled, "Blast that bird bath!"

He came furtively toward the car. Over a shoulder he toted a bulky bag. He did not see me. Before stepping around the corner of his garage and into the dim gleam of his porch light he stopped and reconnoitered.

I was in a good spot to watch. The rain-dribbled windshield screened me. Mister President set down his burden and strolled into the light. His sudden transformation from skulking to strolling was superb.

He looked across the street and up the street and down the street. He held out his hand, as though he had just discovered it was raining, though rain had been falling for an hour and he was dripping. Then, still supposing he had not been seen, he ducked back into the darkness, emerged with his burden and with one swoop opened the back door of the car and heaved it in.

It landed on the floor, and there was the unmistakable thump of duck decoys. Of course, he saw me then, and in the dark I caught the twinkle of his eye by the expression of his voice: "I ain't done nothing, have I?"

"Nothing," I echoed, for it is a rule of the Association that the Old Man's wish is the membership's law.

"All you saw me do was come through Norm's yard from Carl's house with a sack. Isn't that right? Answer me now!"

"Yes, sir," I agreed most solemnly.

"There might have been a body in the sack?"

"Yes, sir."

"There might have been fifty pounds of pine knots from Carl's garage?"

"Yes, sir!"

"Or there might have been half a bale of hay in that sack?"

"Even a whole bale."

"Fine. Just fine," said the President of the Old Duck Hunters. "I take it, then, you are ready to swear that you never saw me steal Carl's decoys?"

"Your honor," I replied, "his decoys are not worth stealing."

"I suppose," he said, "the only kind of decoys worth stealing are those highfalutin, brand-new jobs of yours—the ones you keep in separate bags so's not to ruffle those wooden feathers." He snorted. "The boosters in that ragged gunny sack which you did not see me steal are ducks! Ducks with a past. Ducks with a reputation. Not a shot hole in 'em. Old ducks—and anybody knows wild ducks like old decoys better'n new ones."

Mister President was off on a pet subject. He has long maintained that the wooden creatures, many times painted and patched, are superior to more modern decoys, no matter how perfect. He holds that "there is something about those old boys—they've got character."

"Anyway," I said, "I did not see you steal them. I am prepared to swear to it."

"Heaven help us," he replied. "The boy is going to be a hypocrite like me."

"Yes, sir!"

"Shut up!" he barked.

He went up the four steps of his back porch and into the house, where I knew he was saying farewell to Mrs. President. I knew, sitting in the car, that he was stooping under the big lamp to kiss her good-by and that she put down the evening paper to pat his shoulder, and that then he was standing in the archway, grinning at her, and she was saying, "Goodby, you dear old fool."

Now he was beside me in the car, wearing the old brown mackinaw with the threadbare shawl collar. I nursed the big car carefully through the drenched streets of town. The thing has the power of a jeep in low gear. It has creaked and swayed and hauled the Old Duck Hunters to many a rendezvous with bluebill and mallard.

"I've had my eye on Carl's ducks for years," he explained. "He keeps them in his basement. I saw my chance the other day. His wife—you know how squeamish she is—caught a mouse in a trap. I was in the yard and she hollered over to me.

"That was my cue. I went down in Carl's basement to remove said mouse, and at the same time I just opened a handy window and hoisted that sack of decoys right out under a lilac bush."

"Why didn't you ask Carl if he'd loan them?" I suggested, though I knew better.

The President stuffed new tobacco on old pipe tobacco and replied: "Did you ever ask a man to loan his pet fly rod —or his oldest carpet slippers?"

"But your own decoys are as old—likely better."

He contemplated that not more than a split second before answering: "Listen, when you were young didn't you ever steal a watermelon?"

The fact is, of course, that Mr. President's 30-odd ancient decoys, born and raised on the St. Clair River flats, are genuine museum pieces, hoary and racked with age—just the decoys for a man like Mr. President, or any man.

"I'll admit," he allowed, "that Carl's may be a bit younger than mine. But they look good to me. Dang it, they look like old man MacDougal's apples used to look hanging over the side of his picket fence."

He did not add that he and Carl have waged lusty feuds for years. They have kept the whole neighborhood in an expectant ferment. There was the time Mister President set the rabbit snares to exterminate a family of bark-loving snow-shoe hares. The snares were not a success, but Carl saw to it that a stuffed wildcat was caught in one and a fur buyer's catalogue in another.

So it has gone, with Mister President claiming a signal victory as of the Sunday afternoon he engineered the beer truck up to Carl's front door. Carl was entertaining the Christian Endeavor Society. He is a teetotaler.

Occasionally Mister President and Carl hunt together, but not as often as formerly. I feel partly responsible for breaking up this relationship since I included myself as a member of the President's family. Carl himself has often accused me: "I saw him first, didn't I?"

We drove south through the rain. Mister President pointed out I was wrong in surmising that the rain might turn to snow. "Wind is off Lake Superior. It'd have to switch to the northwest to make snow this time of year."

We stopped at a certain log house by a big lake and put up for the night. It is my house, but you would never know it. Most people think of it as the President's. I made a snack of tea and toast while Hizzoner hauled in Carl's stolen treasures and went over their anchor ropes.

Those decoys were wondrous objects. Some were blue-winged teal, some coots, and some were obviously intended to represent mallards. A surrealist would have adored them. Viewing them, I thought longingly of my own exact imitation jobs, correct in so far as it is possible for an artist (not I!) to make them.

"Ah," said Mister President, surveying his loot. "Ah." He stroked them and patted them and snugged their anchor ropes. "Look at that redhead," he said. "Ever see a better shaped head? Round as an apple just above the eyes. And look at this canvasback! See how its maker shaped the bill? Aquiline, by George, the way a canvasback bill is supposed to be."

It was no time for me to butt in. Secretly, however, I decided that if any ducks decoyed to them in the morning it would be because they were delegates to an All Nations convention of ducks.

He arranged them handily in the car for the morning getaway. We slung a boat on top of the dripping car, against the morning business, and before I had finished washing the tea dishes Mister President was sound asleep under the scarlet blankets, the alarm clock close to his ear—the clock that runs only when placed face downward.

It seemed only a matter of seconds later when a voice roared in my ear, "Ro-o-o-l-l out, you 'jacks! Bacon's in the pan and fifteen miles to go!"

No mortal can be so wide awake as the President of the Old Duck Hunters at 4 A.M. At that time, when life is supposed to be at lowest ebb, he is at a vigorous peak. I think it is because he gauges every tomorrow as calculatingly as he gauges the range of a suspicious mallard. At any rate, he is a picture of leisured organization, come morning.

The bacon must be crisp and drained on brown paper. The coffee must be egg coffee, velvet-smooth. The eggs must be barely caressed on their tops with melted butter. The bread must be twice toasted, once to dry it and once to stiffen it into toast all the way through.

There was no time to wash the dishes. Our route led around the lake in the dark rain to the narrow road running south to the Totogatic flowage. This man-made lake in Sawyer County, Wisconsin, has established new and inviting feeding grounds for waterfowl. Some say it is ugly because of the drowned trees. The Old Duck Hunters hold that beauty is as beauty does.

The road was a worry. The high-wheeled old powerhouse of a car needed all it had to get through the clay at hill bottoms and plow up the next incline.

A charming road, this. It penetrates one of the wildest

sections of Wisconsin. We went past Smoky Hill fire-tower, past Roy Harmon's deer-hunting rendezvous, over the stone bridge that Hank Koehler built across the Ounce River. Past the deer stand where Pat nailed old yellowhorns, past the Porcupine Hotel (another deer camp), past the big stand of hardwood, and so to the Nelson Dam at the foot of the 1,800-acre Totogatic flowage.

Here, the Totogatic River was dammed, so that its hemlock-stained waters were backed up four miles. It is one of four similar water-retention projects in this county, but hunting and fishing men look upon it as a comparatively new field of operations.

Tamarack, popple, pine and spruce were flooded when the waters rose. They stand there now, drowned and dead. The stark trees, with acres and acres of bog, offer the men of waterfowling endless opportunity for cover. Early in the season it is mallards and teal, of course. Later the bull-chested bluebills seem unable to resist the sprawling flowage.

Functioning systematically, the Old Duck Hunters soon had everything in the boat, and were rowing, a pair of oars apiece, south and east to a narrows. Halfway to the place, Mister President called a halt to listen. His sharp ears had caught an outboard's roar above the sound of our rowing. It was coming our way.

"It might be someone wanting our blind," he said without delay. "Bear down on those oars, boy!"

We beat the outboard. As we were splashing blocks overboard the motorboat hesitated before us in the dark. Its occupant sized up the situation and sped on, setting up a half mile away.

"This here blind," the President explained once we were in it, "is the best on the flowage. That boy who tried to make it is smart, though. He's picked the second best place."

Daylight came somberly over the gray waters. It thrust slantwise through the dead tamaracks. But long before it was time to shoot, the President had made his inevitable second visit to the decoys to rearrange them, as is his way.

"They look different once you're in the blind," he said as he climbed back in.

The wind was at our backs. Before us was a horseshoe of decoys, with the toe of the shoe twenty-five yards from the blind. One arm of the shoe stretched in a long string straight out into deeper water, so that ducks coming in would be guided by the "teasers" over the pocket of decoys which formed the toe of the shoe.

Daylight grew. So did those decoys of Carl's. Some of them looked like gargoyles, and some just looked like tomfool decoys. A more motley assortment was never spread, with the possible exception of Mister President's own monstrosities.

"I wish," he whispered, "that I'd brought Min and Bill to give 'em just a lee-e-e-tle more oomph."

Min and Bill are two caricatures of decoys, allegedly mallards, named for a cozy pair of live decoys that the O.D.H.A. owned in other days. Min has had at least ten coats of paint plastered over her, and Bill has a fissure down the center of his solid back that you can stick a finger into—"but they're a hundred years old, and game to the core."

The lack of Min and Bill worried Mister President until a pair of speculating black ducks sailed by, turned—with astonishment, I think—and flailed right over Carl's comic-strip boosters.

"I told you!" the President exulted. "Those decoys of Carl's are all right. You can't beat old decoys!"

I retrieved the two blacks with the boat, readjusted a couple more of Carl's frauds according to Mister President's shouted directions, hid the boat and climbed back in.

Business was good. To be sure, many a wary black and mallard flared from the stand; but when I complained that it was the fault of the decoys, the President said it was because I had kicked a shell box, or wiggled my head, or because my side of the blind had too much cover sticking up high. "And ducks don't like you like they do me, anyway."

The President described it as "a nice steady day." The advance guard of the bluebill flight was in, tempted to tarry by flowing smartweed, which was at a great peak that season. "Within a matter of days, or perhaps a week, the whole pack of bluebills will be here," the President pointed out.

"That won't be the best shooting," he added. "That kind of shooting is too good. You get your ten ducks too soon, and then you got to go home and put on storm-windows. That's what a conscience will do for you."

It was my job to slide the hidden skiff off the bog and retrieve the ducks that fell. I like it. The Association has decreed that such work shall always be laid out for the rank and file. Mister President swore that day that the job was a privilege. "You just drag that heavy boat off the bog in order to get warmed up, while I've got to sit here and freeze."

The rain kept up. Northeasters from Lake Superior have a way of blowing for three days. It would abate, and then begin again. The President had been right. No snow fell.

We ate our sandwiches, and the flight fell off. It fell off so noticeably that Mister President, standing full length in the blind, could not "look ducks," a technique he claims is very sporting. His idea is that if he exposes himself prominently a duck going by will think there is a fool in the blind and whirl in to make sure.

We stuck it out. At quitting time, when I waded out to recapture Carl's decoys, there was a fair limit of birds. The unknown occupant of the blind down the shore called it quits shortly after. He had done very well, we knew, from watching his birds fall. He came putt-putting in at the Nelson Dam as we were hoisting our boat on to the car.

"I'll be dinged!" said Mr. President. "It's Carl!"

"I never saw nothing," I reminded him.

We helped Carl with motor and skiff. Mister President was especially solicitous of his friend and neighbor. He exclaimed over the nice bag of ducks he had. He said over and over again it was a dog-gone shame we hadn't known who it was up the shore—"then we could have hunted together."

"By George," he said, "it's like old times, getting together like this."

Carl was equally pleased. He said, "By George, it's been a grand day, even if it did rain and I'm wet to the skin."

And so Mister President invited him back to our bailiwick where, over steaming cups of quick coffee, they hearkened back to other days. The two of them killed at least a hundred sharptails on my hearth. They stood again, as of yore, in the snowy cut-over in deer season, agreeing that any man who lit a fire for warmth was a softie.

"I allus hold," Carl declared, "that even a hemlock-bark fire scares deer, even if it doesn't give off smoke."

They were a precious pair. I left them to stir up a hot meal in the kitchen. Through the window I noted that Carl's boat had slipped sideways in its trailer cradle. I went out to straighten it and pushed his decoy sack back into the center of the boat, where it would ride. The old cord closing the sack broke, and a decoy rolled into the bottom of the boat.

It was Mister President's Bill, crack in the back and all. Dear old Min was only a few layers below him. The whole sack held nothing but Mister President's aging decoys—the silly coots, the skinny teal, the multicolored redheads. All of them were there.

I switched the sacks to the proper owners then and there, and I went back inside and poured those two old frauds the biggest, hottest plates of lamb stew you ever saw. They sat there, chewing the rag and sopping their bread in the stew and hunting and fishing and agreeing it was a fine thing, indeed, there was somebody around this camp to wash the dishes and sweep the floor for a man.

Carl departed in the rain, full of hot stew. I got to him as he shoved off, after the President had said his last farewell and trooped back to the fire.

"Where," I demanded, "did you get those decoys I just found in your boat?"

"As long as you know," he said, "I went right in and burglarized them. I did it the day I happened to look out a basement window and saw mine under that lilac bush. There was only one man in the world who would try that; so I went over one morning when nobody was home and just swiped his."

He drove off, but not before I had assured him that his own precious fakes had been restored.

Back inside, Mister President was vastly pleased with himself. "You don't know nothing then?" he quizzed.

"Not a thing."

"I really like those ducks of Carl's. He didn't catch on, did he?"

"Didn't have an inkling."

The President of the Old Duck Hunters' Association settled down for a snooze, but before he dropped off he announced, "It takes an old fool to fool an old fool."

"I was trembling. I can't take 'em without quaking. They get right down under me, and turn flip-flops inside. . . . I have caught more trout than I deserve to catch. And always and forever, the good ones like this fellow put me on edge, send me hippity-hopping to a boulder or the bank to sit down and gather my wits."

9

Put this in other words. MacQuarrie is telling us that those who cannot recreate pleasure time after time in the same degree are the most unfortunate among mortals. Here is the direct statement of his main message. Appreciate! Enjoy! Contentment is everywhere if only we can extract it.

"You are as relaxed, physically and mentally, as you will ever be. The river has reached out like an old friend and made a place for you. You pack a leisurely pipe, and the water about you is lit for a minute, the match hisses in the river and the babbling mystery of the night deepens."

Sweet savoring of life. But expect no such poetic expression from Mr. President. *"One thing I can't figger out,"* he calls across the deepening shadows of the river. *"How can a Scotch Presbyterian like you enjoy anything that's so much fun?"*

Now, In June

No time is better for trout fishermen than early June. Other months may approach it. They may even excel it now and then. But what I am getting at is that June is the best time for trout fishermen, as well as trout fishing.

Take the President of the Old Duck Hunters' Association, Inc., for instance. This symbolic angler said to me one night in knee-deep June in his back yard, "I can tell by the smell in the air I am going trout fishing tomorrow."

It was a good smell. Flowers were coming up out of brown earth. Insects hummed. The neighborhood was suffused with the odors of lush June. You smelled it and, smelling it, wondered if you would take those stuffy waders tomorrow or just an old pair of pants for wading.

"Yes, sir," said Mr. President, "I can smell trout tonight. I can smell 'em along towards tomorrow night on the Namakagon below Cable. I will just put me in there at Squaw Bend for maybe not more 'n an hour or two. It'll be dusk when the wind dies; so the mosquitoes will help me change flies.

"First, I will eat supper in the car. I will be pretty lazy about it. I will not be hurried, you understand? I will set there a spell. I'll bet I hardly move a muscle until I hear the

105

first whippoorwill. Then after a bit I will jump in below the county trunk bridge and tempt providence and the good brown trout of the Namakagon with large, unscientific, come-sundown flies. That is what I will do."

Imagine a man in this feverish age, twenty-four hours beforehand, declaring exactly what he will do twenty-four hours hence, come what will as to weather, business or the current status of his sciatic rheumatism.

"Yep," he reiterated there in his back yard, "I will drive down past McKinney's drug-store there in Cable and over to the river, and just as I'm arriving at Squaw Bend four cars with Illinois license plates will be pulling out. These will be city fishermen who don't know any better than to fish for Namakagon browns in broad daylight. They will be sore at the river. They will tell me there ain't a brown in the river—never was! They will go away from there, leaving it to me just when I want it, as the fishing gets good.

"I'm danged if I can figger out what trout fishermen these days are thinking about. They start at 10 A.M., after a good night's rest and a leisurely breakfast. They fish until the six-o'clock whistle, and wonder why they don't get 'em. People like that are not entitled to catch trout. To catch trout, you got to suffer and learn."

He carried out the next day's schedule to a T. He abandoned his business at three, and one hour later came up my front walk in khaki trousers, his eyes snapping. I was only half ready. There had been a slight argument at our house. My wife, who is Mister President's daughter, just sort of hung around and looked abused while I picked up my stuff. That can unnerve people like me.

The President took in matters at a glance and yelped: "For heaven's sake, woman! Get away from that man! Can't you see he ain't soaked his leaders yet?"

Think of it! A man who can talk like that and make it stick! Picking up the final odds and ends, however, I won-

dered for the hundredth time why he could not command
so imperiously in his own house, where he achieves his ends
by other means—obsequiousness, if not downright chicanery. It's a smart man who knows when he's licked.

"Trout fishing is not like drinking beer," he lectured as
the car sped south and east. "It's more like sipping champagne. A good beer drinker just sits him down and lays into it.
You hear the first one splash. But you just sip champagne.
You take a tiny leetle bit and smack your lips.

"So with trout. You don't want too many. You want to
get the stage all set. You look ahead and figger out every
move. You will not be rushed. You are not after a bait of
fish. If you are, you would go down to the St. Croix and
jerk the derned teeth out of smallmouths. What you are
after is to fool a trout, or maybe four or five.

"I'm for filling frying-pans, you understand. But only
now and then. More often I'm for picking out a trout so
smart he thinks of running for the legislature. There he is,
living under the bank by daylight and sneering at the guys,
who waste their time working over him when the sun is
high. My idea of perfection is to give that guy a dose of
sprouts—to teach him a lesson he won't forget, if I can't
creel him."

"Then you have some places in mind—"

"I'll thank you not to poke into other people's affairs and
also to stay away from that hole two hundred yards below
the town road, where the big dead stump sticks out into
the river."

"Agreed. In return, will you avoid the fast rip below the
island?"

"Why should I fool with half-pounders?" he snorted.
"Your ten-cent rips are secure against trespass."

We drove under Cable's gorgeous pines, past McKinney's
drug-store, which has seen more big browns than most drug-

stores, past the sawmill, and thence to the Namakagon at Squaw Bend, which is some place.

"Not exactly slightly known, however," Mister President replied when I raised the question. "Too dog-gone well known. But, happily, not intimately to fishermen who will play its own game."

"Like who?"

"Like me. Me, I wouldn't come down here a-whipping and a-lashing this crick in broad daylight. Oh, mebbe I would on an overcast, windy day. And how many of those do we get in a season? Me, I'd come down here either first thing in the morning or last thing at night. I'd rather do this than mow the lawn, I would. . . ."

He wheeled the car across a shallow, dry ditch, and it settled on low, hard ground, off the road. Twenty feet away the Namakagon journeyed by in the last direct rays of the sun. He broke out sandwiches and coffee and forbade me to move out of the car "until the time is ripe."

There was the dear old river. And sure enough, two disgusted fishermen coming to their car, parked near by, who answered a hail with "You can have our share of it."

"Imagine!" snorted the President. "The exalted conceit of people who will fish this creek on a day the sky is so bright it isn't blue, but white! There they go, and fair weather after them. Quitting at seven o'clock. You know, I think this present generation of trout fishermen is afraid of the dark!"

Softly comes the night along the Namakagon. Born in cold, crooked-shored Namakagon Lake, it curves south and west to the St. Croix, its upper reaches trout water, its lower reaches smallmouth water almost on a par with the St. Croix itself.

There it was, just beyond the car windows, gray and ropy in the growing dusk. It ran under the county trunk bridge, surged to the right and lost itself around the corner, where there is a grand series of rips. You just look at that kind of river in June and want to plump right into it.

Not, however, when the President is in charge. We sat and munched. In that far northern corner of Wisconsin, darkness comes slowly in early June. That is a great help to deliberate evening campaigners. Those twilights were made for trout fishermen. They give you time, the President says, "to square off at it."

It was a night to remember, and the Old Duck Hunters remember many such and are properly thankful. June along the Namakagon is a month of heavy perfumes and many birds. No stretch of the Namakagon in the Cable-Seeley country offers more than the Squaw Bend territory.

Trout waters can be very personal places. The best trout streams are the ones you grow up with and then grow old with. Eventually they become like a familiar shotgun, or a faithful old setter, or a comfortable pair of shoes. You develop a profound affection for them, and you think maybe before you die you will even understand a little about them.

We went downstream, he on the right bank, I on the left. At this putting-in place, high above the right bank, stretches the level top of an old logging railroad grade. The light was waning in the west, and the top of this embankment cut off the sky like a knife. Below this ran the churning river, far noisier and more mysterious than it had been an hour before.

Certainly you must know how it is to come to a place like this. A place you know well. A place where you are on intimate terms with the smallest boulders, where yonder projecting limb once robbed you of a choice fly, where from beneath the undercut banks the big ones prowl by night to claim the larger morsels of the darkness.

Strange and utterly irresistible are such places to trout fishermen. There you had hold of a good one. Here you netted a smaller one. Down beyond the turn in the pool below the old snag pile you lost still another. The spell of approaching night silenced the President, but not for long.

"One thing I can't figger out," he said finally. His voice came to me from a point downstream, drifting over the purring waters in the sweet June air, "How can a Scotch Presbyterian like you enjoy anything that's so much fun?"

He vanished in the gloom like some wise and ancient spirit of the river. I heard his wader brogues nick a rock as he stumbled, heard him cuss softly and then the river took me in. . . .

Though it is early June, the mosquitoes are not bad. One of those rare nights when the pesky hordes fail to discover you there in mid-river. The temperature had dropped quickly from a sunlit 80 or so to below 70, and you know it will be a night for blankets. You know, too, as the water laps at waders that it is the cool, kindly hand of night which chills your river every twenty-four hours and makes it livable for trout.

You are as relaxed, physically and mentally, as you will ever be. The river has reached out like an old friend and made a place for you. You pack a leisurely pipe, and the water about you is lit for a minute, the match hisses in the river and the babbling mystery of the night deepens.

The current plucks at your knees. Your fingers feel in the darkness for the familiar shapes of bass-sized trout flies. A whim will decide which one. From long experience you have learned to hold fingers toward the western sky as you bend on your choice.

What to do? Work the right bank down, foot by foot, with the short, efficient line of the after-sunset angler? Or cover all the water methodically, persistently?

Plop! A Namakagon brown has decided the issue for you. He is downstream maybe as much as fifty yards, and a good fat plop it is. Just the kind of trout you would expect to come prowling out from the snags on a cool June evening.

You know it is the careless fling of a worthy brown, and you are pretty sure he will look at something big and buggy, that he is confident and bellicose.

But just a minute now! You've tried these fish before in the near dark. They come quickly and they go quickly. Once pricked, they standeth not upon the ceremony of their departing. You tighten up a bit. Browns, though more foolhardy by night, can still be very chancy. You do, however, reach around and feel for the net handle, but quickly make personal amends to whatever fishing gods there be. You know it does not pay to be cocky. You know you must study to be humble and alert.

You take it easy in getting to a spot upstream from the fish. You get over to the left bank for your little stalk, and you lift your feet high and put them down easily. You study the vague outline of the branches with which you will have to contend in casting. You take long, hard drags at the little blackened pipe, so that the bowl glows hot. You are on edge and ready. You get within thirty-five feet of the place and wait. . . .

Plop! Good! He is not frightened. You false-cast with the big fly, wondering how to show it to him. A slack-line drift down over him? Or cross-current cast and a smart retrieve? You decide on the former. It will disturb the water less, and you can come back to the fussier cast later.

You lengthen line, and you know your fly is going over his window. Nothing. Again and again you cast, letting it drift below him and out into midstream. And you retrieve each time carefully, so as not to whip his top water and frighten him. Still nothing. He isn't seeing it.

Very well. You have covered all corners of his window with the dead floating fly. You have shown him Business No. 1, and he wants none of it. Very well. Now for action, à la bass stream. Zip—zip—zip! The fly is brought back over his window in short jerks.

Ka-doong! That was the medicine. He's got it. He's fast and he's heavy and he's going places.

Now, for Pete's sake, take it easy. The leader is sound and the stream is free of stuff, except for that undercut bank. He is bucking like a mule. You strip in a couple of feet, tentatively, and exult at your strategy in showing him an actionable fly, something struggling and toothsome.

He's certainly husky. Those Namakagon busters are built like tugboats. He's sidewise now, below you, in midstream, giving you the works. He has broken water a couple times. He rushes you and you strip in like mad, letting the retrieved line fall where it may in the current.

And then after you have given him Mister President's "dose of sprouts," and you reach around and feel the hickory handle of the net. . . .

Like many another after-dark brown on the Namakagon, this one was a good pound and a half. I did not see him until he was in the net, and that is unusual. Generally you see living flashes of fleshy brown out there in the gloom. He was reddish and thick and cold as ice as I removed the fly, tapped him on the head and slid him into the wide, deep jacket pocket I use for a creel.

I was trembling. I can't take 'em without quaking. They get right down under me, and turn flip-flops inside. The pipe was out. The stripped line was bellied downstream. The fly was chewed. It was a pattern evolved by a friend whose stamping ground is the surging river Wolf. A few of its devotees gave it a name a year back—Harvey Alft's Non-pareil—and it has stuck.

I went over and sat on a boulder near the bank. Just one trout—and all that fuss. I sat and wondered, as all men have, if the day would ever come when I could take so small a fraction of a trout stream's population and not develop a galloping pulse.

I have caught more trout than I deserve to catch. And

always and forever, the good ones like this fellow put me on edge, send me hippity-hopping to a boulder or the bank to sit down and gather my wits.

Another pipeful helped settle things. I thought, sitting there, another bold trout might betray himself by leaping, but none did. I tested the leader, smoked out the pipe and went back upstream by the left bank. Now the first plan of campaign would be in order—fish the right bank like a machine. Swish-swish. That was the only sound there in the dark as the Nonpareil sailed back and out, back and out. Maybe there would be one or two right in close to the bank, just outside the protecting roots.

There was. Indeed there was. Another golden-bellied Namakagon brown mouthed Harvey Alft's Nonpareil with sure determination and made for midstream and faster water. He was smaller, but lively. I horsed him a bit. You are permitted to do that when you are building up to a brace. A pair is so much better than a loner. Two more were netted through the methodical casting toward the right bank, out from which they lay feeding. And there is little excuse for repeating the old, old story.

It was getting on toward 10 P.M., which is the time you quit on trout streams in Wisconsin. I moved downstream to the sacred precincts of Mister President's pool. The whippoorwills were in a dither. A deer splashed at the stream bank and snorted back through the brush. The flat top of the old logging grade was now lit by the stars.

I was proud of my four fish. I showed them to him. He said they were fish that would disgrace no man's skillet. He was sitting on the bank in the dark. His glowing cigar end attracted me. He was a little weary, and I felt a little guilty when he pounded me on the back and then said he had nothing—"but I had hold of one—the one!"

Nothing for Mister President. I do not like to wind up

trout trips with him that way. And, in all conscience, I seldom do!

We followed the bank back to the car and pulled off our waders. It was just ten o'clock. He slumped a little over the wheel, for he was beaten and he was tired. And then, before he stepped on the starter, he rolled down a window and took a good, long sniff of the Namakagon's June aroma.

"You know," he said, "I can tell by the smell in the air I am going trout fishing tomorrow."

"I wish I could say that my buck came through. It would make the story so much better." But the buck doesn't come. And the story couldn't be much better. Or more revealing.

For it is a story of horrendous failure. Mishap. Misadventure. Miscalculation. No deer. No bear. Hard work gone for naught. Exhaustion. Plans awry. Defeat. In other words, the common fabric of life.

But are the Old Duck Hunters dismayed? Do they give up? Hah! *"We hold there is no end to the things a man can do outdoors in all seasons. Ducks, certainly, and geese and deer and rabbits and pheasants—and trout! The Old Duck Hunters, lacking other pressing business, get their fun out of building brush piles for cottontails and planting pine trees for cover."*

Dismay these characters? Hardly. Their fun is infallible. Not only are they the actors in their manufactured dramas, they are also the audience. If the play turns out tragic, they can applaud their simulated sorrow. If comic, the laughter is for real.

And the important thing? Why, insuring that a new play is always waiting to command their talent.

10

The Great Bear Hunt

The President of the Old Duck Hunters' Association, Inc., smote a mosquito and said suddenly, "I know how to get one!"

"Let me in on it. All we've got is four walleyes."

"Tain't fish," said he. How odd, I thought, for we were fishing. "It's bear!"

"Howzzat again?"

"Big black bears. I mind the time George Ruegger trapped one right in this country that went 525 pounds dressed."

I reeled in my mud minnow and spinner to listen.

"I never killed a bear," he explained, "and I need a rug. We've got so many bear the state is opening special seasons on 'em to protect farm stock."

"Now—about the plan?" I prompted.

"Just before a bear holes up he roams the country looking for a den to suit him. Why not fix up some dens so luxurious a bear can't help but go into them? First bear sees the den tumbles in, draws the covers up under his chin and falls asleep. Then come bear season in late fall, you go out and look up the dens!"

I made a tactical error—I laughed. I said it reminded me of the tale from Canada which has it that the way to get a bear is to mix a gallon of molasses with a quart of rum

117

and leave the jug on a bear trail. Then you just go out and
pick up the shameless bear and carry him home.

Mister President glared me down. "It was people just
like you who said Whitney's cotton-gin would never work!"

"But your Honor, a housing project for bears—"

"Row me ashore, I got to see Hank."

I cleaned the pike. Hizzoner drove away, raising dust. I
fried fish, boiled potatoes, fixed a salad, brewed tea. Mister
President returned with Hank. They came down the hill
to the shack arm in arm, Hizzoner talking, Hank listening.

Henry F. Koehler is a power-house of a man, good woodsman, logger, mechanic. He and Mister President go together like Swiss on rye. There is something about Hank
that reminds you of a bear—a great big, long-armed, curly-
headed bear, full of human juices and good-will to mankind.
If there are men who could wrestle bears, Hank would be
among them.

They discussed as they dined.

"Can't see why it won't work," Hank allowed.

"We'll work in north of the fire lane," said Mister President.

"Make the dens under old windfall roots and let the
leaves drift in for bedding."

"We'll hire a bulldozer if we have to!"

I erred once more by asking if they had figured on in-
stalling steam heat. From then on the bear hunters showed
me no mercy. Mister President asked Hank if he recalled
the day I missed a standing buck at forty paces. Did Hank
remember? Oh, my!

"I saw that buck myself from the hill in back of him.
There's Gordie and there's the buck standing so's you could
tie all four legs together with a foot of string. I saw him up
with his gun. He shot two foot over him, and the buck went
thirty foot on the first jump!"

How they remembered, those two—while I did the dishes.

"You mind the time, Hank," Mister President recalled, "when he tried to find the beaver ponds over back of Charlie Warner's?"

"And got lost?"

"Yes, and us up all night looking for him."

"Yes," Hank went on, "and there was that time he dropped his end of the boat on the portage and punched a four-inch hole in the planking, and us with five miles of water to cover and it near dark."

"A man of that stamp should be doubting that we can persuade bears to den up where we want them," thundered the President of the Old Duck Hunters.

When I had dried the last dish, when I had put the night log on the fireplace, when the loons on the lake were quavering of rain, Hank departed for home, but not before he agreed vigorously when Mister President declared, "Furthermore, he's an awful cook!"

Mind you, this was in August, several years ago, and not in late November, when the bear season in Wisconsin ran coincidentally with the deer season.

Early next morning Hank and Mister President went off together in Hank's pick-up, loaded with digging tools. Late that evening they came back to consume the walleyes I had caught. You'll hardly believe it when I say that Hizzoner had Hank so bear-minded that when he washed up before supper he said, "Pardon me while I wash my front paws."

From my hideout in the kitchen I timidly asked what the two comrades had achieved.

Ignoring my query, Mister President rendered his thrice daily benediction upon the junior membership of the association: "That boy's an awful cook."

"And how!" Hank agreed.

Eventually it came out, though they were not inclined to

include me in on their project. "He wouldn't understand bear den engineering if we showed him blueprints," said Mister President.

But, as I say, I caught the drift of the developments from their conversation. They had created some dozen bear dens—five off the fire lane, three more in the big Norway, and five dandies south of the pot-hole lake.

"The bear that turns down those holes wouldn't be happy in the Waldorf Astoria," Mister President declared.

I did not see the cabin again until snow fell, on the eve of the deer-bear season. It was dry, crisp snow, I remember, and as I walked down the hill with rifle and duffle bag I hoped the bear hunters would be there ahead of me.

They were. Peeking in a window, I saw Hizzoner pacing and orating before the fireplace and Hank as raptly attentive as he could possibly be, considering that he was tapping the cover of a snoose box, trying to lay in a quid without letting Mister President think he was being impolite. With ear to the window, I listened to the conversation going on inside.

"He'll land here some time tonight," said Mister President, "him and that fancy rifle. He got somebody to put a telescope on it. Imagine! He'll try to get us to forget the bear hunt and go after deer. He'll likely want to shove north into the Marengo River country, 'way below Ashland, not that the chance of getting a deer there is any better than here, but just because he likes the look of it."

"Well, sir, we'll let him go his way."

"You're dern right!"

Hank agreed, slipping the snoose into a convenient bulge behind his lower lip.

"And we'll go get us a bear or two!"

I pushed in the door with the end of the duffle bag. "Bear hunters, I greet you."

"The bum cook is with us again!" announced Mister President.

Hank stowed my gear in my bedroom and Mister President shoved a camp stew to the hottest lid on the kitchen range.

I turned in early, for I had come quite a way. The last thing I heard was Hank: "We can't miss!"

The bear hunters were up ahead of me. Mister President presided over a gallon or so of steaming oatmeal, some five acres of scrambled eggs with bacon, and a pile of toast about so tall. This amount of provender would be sufficient for an ordinary hunting camp of ten men. It is always provided in such quantity by the Old Duck Hunters when Hank is on hand. I will match Hank Koehler as a table boy with any North Woods gourmet, excepting possibly George Perkins, the Canadian guide who was present when a world-record muskie was collected, and who, I testify, once schlerped up three cans of peaches just for dessert. The physical strength possessed by the Perkinses and the Koehlers requires fueling.

Would the bear hunters, at the last moment, change their plans and hunt deer with me?

You know the answer. Mister President, fairly skipping with confidence, asserted, "I am not going to take after deer in a country where a man can get him a bear."

Hank put in his nickel's worth: "Shucks! Between here and Alaska I've killed mebbe fifty deer. Might just as well have been five hundred if I'd wanted to."

"We ought to get at least two bears out of a dozen dens," calculated Mister President.

"You can have the biggest," said Hank, always magnanimous.

"Nope. We'll toss a coin."

They even knew where they'd get their bearskins tanned—by an Indian woman of the neighborhood who does superlative work. Hank opined that he would not retain the skull on his rug. "Just something to stumble over in the dark."

"We'll be back by noon," said Mister President. "Have your camera ready, my boy."

Away they went in Hank's pick-up, its cleated tires raising the snow, which had reached a depth of four inches. I poured a contemplative cup of coffee. I was beginning to wonder if maybe they weren't on the right track. For a moment I regretted that I had not gone along with them. Then I remembered that they had not invited me. Since that first day, pike fishing, when I had snickered, Mister President had counted me out, and definitely!

The snow had stopped falling when I set out, and daylight was spreading. I headed across the frozen Middle Lake with a place in mind where deer use both sides of a thoroughfare between the lakes. The outlook was not bright. Still-hunting on opening day with more than 100,000 in the Wisconsin woods is a gamble. The drive is more certain. Still it's a nice feeling a man gets in the November woods—being on his own with a rifle.

To be sure, the three of us, working together, could have staged some neat little drives through cover we all knew well. In the course of the day we could have worked out four or five likely areas, with Mister President doing the standing and Hank and I the driving. The Old Man is a champion at freezing on a stump.

I worked out the thoroughfare as best I could, alternately standing and traveling slowly upwind through the shaggy bottoms. I came close once, via an unintentional drive to me. A noisy crew of drivers swept through jack-pine highland and pushed out a good buck with a doe. There was a chance for one hasty shot as the buck sailed into the bottom cover, but I knew I was over him and then some. The drive came on. They would note the buck's tracks and try again to shove him into the open. I left the thoroughfare.

I like to travel in the deer woods. The going was nice—

not too much snow. The country was lovely and grim with a promise of more snow. I knew a place.

It is a remnant of big hemlocks, a hundred acres or so, where a man could walk among three-foot trunks 150 years old. I go there often, hunting or not. Once I showed this stand to an old logger of Wisconsin's Chippewa River valley. He put his arms around a big hemlock and bawled. That old-timer knew that the great stands of hemlock in the northern part of the Middle West are gone, probably forever. He knew that the hemlock cannot be regenerated, as the pines can; that this tree is something of a freak among the conifers, a sociable plant which does best in huge stands.

I stood on a rise at the edge of this place and wished Mister President and Hank were there. We could have made a neat little drive, leaving the Old Man behind on the rise as Hank and I made a wide swing and drove up through the big trees. Plenty of opportunity for an open shot, and if we shoved through a buck Mister President, waiting, chilled, with a drop on the end of his nose, would have been a very reliable gent with his .30-30.

I picked a screened spot for a stand, halfway down the rise. A mighty fine place for a man to wait for a deer because of those marvelous hemlocks lifting more than a hundred feet straight up. Something might move through. The herd was on the rampage with all those hunters in the woods.

I ate a sandwich. The afternoon wore on. I ripped hemlock bark from a dead giant and got it to going. The flames died away, and it burned like coal, red and solid and warming.

It began to snow. I wish every deer hunter could spend at least one day in a hemlock stand in the deer season. The light coming down made yellow and purplish patterns on the trees and on the snow. A stark-white weasel with black-tipped tail stalked within five feet of me. Hairy and downy woodpeckers hammered into the bark of the great trees. Chickadees, hanging upside down, studied me.

A doe with twin fawns came by. They passed through without realizing I was there. Ravens croaked high above the big trees. I wish I could say that my buck came through; it would make the story so much better. But he did not come. When the grove was dimming in the dusk, I left and felt that I had had a good day.

Falling snow blew into my face as I back-tracked five miles through the thoroughfare, and thence across the frozen lake. Perhaps the bear hunters would be there waiting for me. Perhaps they would have two shaggy brutes hung on the pole which was spiked to the scrub-oaks.

From the open lake in that last mile of going I saw no gleaming light at the cabin. It was pitch-dark and snowing very hard when I had washed the breakfast dishes and started supper. It was 8 P.M. when I had supper ready—and no bear hunters.

I dined alone, and shoved the food to the back of the range to be kept warm for the bear hunters. The snow was piling up. It piled up so high that season at the opening that half the deer hunters in the country pulled out, whipped.

I worried some, too. Mister President and Hank are woodsmen, be assured of that. I worried anyway.

It was after 9 P.M. when I heard Hank's pick-up roaring through the snow, saw the lights of it coming, and dropped two big fistfuls of tea into boiling water. Two wearier bear hunters never walked into a camp. I wanted to laugh, but you don't laugh when a man as tireless as Hank walks into your camp and stands there, rocking. As for Mister President, he padded across the floor in his gum rubbers and flopped on a studio couch without a word.

I poured hot tea into them, followed by thick camp soup, the kind you have to chew. They had taken nothing with them to eat. Had they not anticipated being back to the cabin at noon with a bear apiece?

There are times in the bush when you do not press a man.

If he is tired, it is well understood by the Old Duck Hunters that the tired man must first be taken care of, that no prying questions be shot at him. It is the logical business of first things coming first. In this case it was a matter of getting something into the stomachs of the bear hunters that would make them believe the world was not all weariness.

Hank came around first. "The pick-up broke down, and we had to fix it. It was the wiring."

After that, misfortune followed misfortune. The right rear tire blew out, a patching job. The windshield wiper quit working. The gas gauge showed low because of the places they drove in low gear.

But they were determined to look at every one of those created bear dens. They had walked "a million miles." They were "too tired to eat." (After two cups of tea apiece they ate like starved springer spaniel pups.) They had gone to all the places—off the fire lane, into the big Norway pines, and south of the pot-hole lake.

That was one night when the lesser member of the ODHA practically put the senior membership to bed. I mean I just turned down the blankets and they fell in. And it was not until they were in their separate beds in one room that I put the $64 question—did we get a bear?

So long as I live I shall never forget the confession of fact which this question reluctantly brought from Mister: "We didn't even find the dens that we made!"

From Hank's bed came the explanation: "The country looks so different after it snows."

I tiptoed away from there to my allotted post in the kitchen. Making rendezvous with the dirty dishes, I snickered, and the Old Man must have heard me, for he yelled: "Hey, bum cook! Come here." He was too tired to rise on an elbow; so I leaned over and he said: "I knocked over a little forkhorn in the big Norway. Take the pick-up and bring him in early. You know where I always hang 'em."

I do believe he was dead asleep before I got out of the room.

In the morning I tightened the chains on Hank's pick-up and brought in the buck, hanging it myself from the pole with block and tackle while the bear hunters slept until noon.

The snow kept coming. The bear hunters revived, and by nightfall, when fourteen inches lay on the level, they agreed that not many deer would be killed in northwest Wisconsin that season. Only an occasional road hunter in that country got his buck that season, as it turned out. It is one thing to hunt on bare ground or light tracking snow; another thing to hunt over fourteen inches of snow.

When I left the bear hunters they were offering no apologies. Had they not given their all in the try? Had not the Old Man knocked over the forkhorn in the Norways? Who was it provided the inch-thick venison steaks? The bear hunters.

I did not get back to the place until the following August. I arrived there with intent to do bodily harm to wall-eyed pike, northern pike, big bluegills and muskellunge. After parking my car on the hill overlooking the shack I went down the gently slanting path. There was the sound of a hammer driving nails into wood.

It was the bear hunters. Hank was laying in a fresh cud of snoose. The President of the Old Duck Hunters' Association was kneeling on the ground, hammering nails into good white pine lumber, freshly planed and sawed.

"We got 'er made big enough," I heard Hank say.

I confronted them. Hank offered me a chew of snoose. The President of the Old Duck Hunters' Association arose from his labors and looked me squarely in the eye: "We're making a bear sled for next fall."

"You are an unregenerate back-slider," said
I to the President of the Old Duck Hunters'
Association, Inc.

"You bet your life I am," he answered
spiritedly.

"You are," I went on, *"a hypocritical rascal
without principle or virtue of any kind in
your mangy hide."*

"Right again," agreed the President.

*"This water is perfect for a dry fly and I'll
stake my reputation on it."*

"Your reputation," the woods rang with his
laughter. *"Shucks, sonny, you ain't got no
reputation. You're a fisherman."*

*Of all the many great moments of MacQuarrie
stories that could not be crammed into this
collection, that exchange cries out for preserva-
tion. It is a fitting pinnacle from which to
leap into* The Little Flight. *For you will therein
achieve even greater heights. Many consider
it one of the all-time great hunting stories.*

11

The Little Flight

In the autumn in the North there comes a time when a few stupid crickets courageously carry on their idle fiddling, but you can never tell, as you drop off to sleep, whether yon shrilling insect will survive the night or shrivel under the frost-whitened grass. It is a time when high noon may find the bees under a full head of steam and the horizon a-glimmer with heat waves, even though the goldenrod is dead and only the purple asters flaunt their color. It is a time when the season offers damning proof that men with calendars know not what they are doing when they split the year into four arbitrary parts.

Some call it Indian summer, that precious interlude before squaw winter, which is the fake winter that comes with snow and gale and is liquidated around Thanksgiving with a real blast from the north. Some call it the tail end of summer; but whatever it is named, there is no place on the calendar for it. It is too heady with autumn scent for August. It is too warm for October.

This is, as much as anything, the wedding of the seasons, the perfect blend of warmth and chill and sun and frost. It is also the time when the first of the migrating ducks marshal their legions and skim away from old homes. Not, of course, on that headlong, hurry-up plunge we call the big

129

flight, but rather on shorter, preliminary jaunts. It is the little flight.

The big flight comes after. It is a compulsory thing, brought about by ice-glazed bays where the rice and wapato and coontails grow. The big one is a stern and frigid business of earlaps and mittens and thrashing arms to keep up circulation. It is the traditional flight that we all know about and read about and look forward to. The little flight is so modest, so untraditional, so unsung, that sometimes it comes through our favorite duck wallows when we least expect it.

But I know a man so firmly grounded in the arts and parts of waterfowling that he could not possibly ignore the little flight, and that man, of course, is the man who is always ready, willing and able—the Honorable President of the Old Duck Hunters' Association, Inc., which stands for incorrigible.

"I tell you," he said to me one early October evening, "there's an early movement of ducks through north Wisconsin and all the Middle Western States that has never been properly recognized."

He was tinkering with the ropes and weights of some thirty of the darnedest-looking decoys ever known—handmade caricatures fashioned of wood, painted and repainted until the stuff lay on like armor. He had acquired this set of boosters by bribery the minute he learned they were a hundred years old and had been used on the St. Clair River flats, near Detroit, before the Civil War.

He would jerk an anchor cord, find it firm, and toss the ancient cheat into the good pile. The infirm and the injured members of this precious flock he doctored with paint, lampblack, putty, lead, weights, and even now and then a bit of a soft pine plug to seal up abdominal fissures.

"Say what you will," he continued, "there is a sneak flight of ducks flying down this way that your season's tail-ender misses completely. Call it just a trickle if you wish.

Still it's a flight. And I don't mean just summer ducks like blue-wing teal and wood ducks. I mean big gray mallards and bigger black mallards and ringbill and widgeon and sprig. The thing is, you've got to hit it right, and you can't do that hunting just week-ends. You might be lucky. And you might not be lucky."

Was there, I inquired, a way a man could tell when this vanguard came along?

"A man would. A good man"—he appraised me—"would have his duck marsh handy by, say fifty miles away, and would have a look at it every day the third week of October, let us say. Yep, that would be the week for these parts. Most of the sky-busters have forgotten about ducks since the locals grew so wary, and a man studying a marsh would know what was coming into it. He'd notice if they increased suddenly, if they traded over different passes; and if they seemed the least bit tamer than the locals, he'd know what they were —visitors."

So the pilgrimage began. First, there was a veritable expedition in which a trailer and two large barrels figured prominently. Also a skiff, which was hidden in the tamarack of a semi-dry swamp facing a mile-long stretch of giant wild rice. The barrels were rolled, dragged and sometimes carried until the President said, "This is the place. Dig!"

One of the barrels was a large, spic-and-span oil drum, which had been washed out with gasoline. The other was an obese hogshead which had once served as a pickle barrel. I have hated dill pickles ever since; so now you know who drew the pickle barrel.

Excavation began in the dry, shifting sand at the edge of the wild-rice bed. The first two feet were easy. Then we hit water, and it was a race to shovel out sand before water came in. We won, but not before the barrels, side by side, had to be pushed and dug and crammed down through the sand and water. In a good, stiff rain they would pop up like a jack-in-the-box, but the Old Duck Hunters go nowhere without shovels, and it was always possible to reseat them.

Such were the blinds. You let yourself down into them and braced your back against the inner walls. A mound of sand around their rims, flush with the ground, was trimmed with the native flora, covering your head. The theory was fine. I got so I could stay in one almost twenty minutes! The President, a patient man, could worm down in, adjust his head cover, light his crooked little pipe and stay there for hours, perfectly comfortable.

Once a visiting hunter stepped into one of these blinds and well-nigh broke a leg. The President told him they were porcupine traps and he had better be careful, because they were sprinkled all over the place. The visiting hunter did not again trespass upon the secret shores of Shallow Bay.

The dedication of those barrels occurred after the opening, a period dedicated by the Old Duck Hunters mostly to creeping up to hidden pot-holes back in the cut-over. The lull had set in. Hunters quit the marshes for other shooting. They were the sky-busters, waiting for the big parade. Ducks, to them, meant a first day and a cold day, and in between not much of anything.

The daily ride to the wild-rice bed continued. When the old maestro couldn't get away, yours patiently undertook the long trip, to report back each night what he had seen come into the marsh over the high hill and through the pass and from down Namakagon River way. The prexy followed these reports diligently, and mostly shook his head. The little flight was not yet in. The trickle had not yet begun.

Then there came a lowering day in the beginning of October's third week and, hearkening to my evening report, Mister President opined there should be something to see next evening—"The paper says it's 15 above at Medicine Hat. No sign of it here, but something will move down in front of that wave. We may even catch a bit of the weather here."

He was right. Next evening, as I surveyed the tawny rice bed of Shallow Bay in the final rays, there was more of a clatter in the center. And there were more birds dropping in. The music of wild mallards is worth listening to anywhere, but never better than when it comes to the ears over an old, familiar duck patch where history has been made. I drove a little faster on the way home to tell him.

Had there been more moving? Were there more birds coming in recklessly, without preliminary swings? Were there, maybe, some bluebills in the rice with the ringbills and the mallards? And teal around yet? The answers all being met with a nod of Mister President's head, he decreed an early start and plenty of shells—"especially for you on those high ones. Me, I'll get along with a couple of boxes."

In the morning we had the marsh to ourselves. If anything, the congress of waterfowl scattered over the marsh had increased during the night. That dove-tailed with the weather, for the Canadian arctic front had hopped over the boundary and was whooping through the Dakotas and Minnesota and north Wisconsin. It was cold, and it was going to get colder. You don't have to look at the weather forecast to know that. Years of watching autumn northwesters in that country replace calculation with instinct.

The marsh wasn't frozen over. It might be in another twenty-four hours. And afterward, if the weather softened, it might open up again and stay open, even that far north, as I have seen it, far into November. This, of course, is unusual, but I have even seen that marsh open in December.

The mile of wind-tossed rice stretched out before us. It was almost broad daylight when we had set out the decoys and adjusted ourselves in the blind. The odor of those long-departed dill pickles penetrated into my heavy blanket coat, and the President whispered across; "I can smell you and the barrel from here. On the way home, if we meet someone, pretend you don't know me."

From behind a screen of twigs we peered out. It was going to be long shooting, he said. "Be sure and mark your birds— the cover is tough. Me, I'll drop mine right at the edge of the decoys."

Would he want to place a little bet on the first duck? Say a good 10-cent cigar with a band on it? Would he? Quick as a snake on a sunny rock he snapped me up. "Make it a box of shells. The rules are, any man may shoot when he's a mind to without tipping off the other guy."

Even while he spoke I noted his eyes were not on me, but were directed through the little curtain of leaves. Hawkeyed, he was watching something in the air. I was too late. The long, lean barrel of his automatic flipped at the boom, and a single greenhead plunged almost into the decoys. He was about to sound a croak of victory, but sank quickly into the barrel and pointed out front.

The shot had brought the marsh alive with tip-up feeders. Blacks and mallards mostly, big devils hovering over the fringed rice, uncertain whether to flop back into the feeding troughs below or pick up and move on. A dozen, too curious, wheeled in close, and there was no time then to lay a bet. They hung in front of us in a 30-mile wind, not close, but close enough. When they had side-slipped away, three more lay out in the rice, and the President reminded me hurriedly that he always shot 1¼-ounce loads and for me not to hand him in payment any piddling ounce loads that I carried around.

Many of the departing ducks fled over the high hill, and soon we could hear the biddies stridently advertising the succulence of this new paradise. We hauled out the skiff and retrieved the down birds, during which Mister President politely requested me to stay down-wind from him—"There's nothing like a dill pickle, though, with a hot dog!"

Anyway, there were other things to occupy us, not to mention the pickle barrel. It was not easy searching out the fallen birds. When it was done and we were adjusted in the blinds, Mister President, sniffing the heavy odor of salt vinegar and cucumbers which emanated from me, said it was a good thing that ducks couldn't smell, else there would be no shooting on the marsh that day. He also said he wished he had a clothes-pin to hang over his nose. There are few idle moments in duck blinds with the President.

Curiosity got the better of the puddlers over the hill, and they began drifting back into the bigger rice bed. The Bible says that the fool returneth to his folly as the dog to his vomit; and while we would be the last to assert that a mallard is a fool, certainly these mallards were not post-graduate locals. Our blinds were perfect, except for the odor which emanated from mine. There was not a sign of anything above ground but natural growth. Not even the old felt hat of Mister President, the band of which was festooned with twigs.

The day wore on, and it rained. It rained, and I missed ducks. I have missed ducks before and will miss them again, but seldom have I missed them like that. These travelers of the little flight had me stopped cold. Maybe, I thought, it was the light one-ounce loads, but light one-ounce loads will kill ducks, and I knew it. So did the President know it. He borrowed a couple and killed a couple of ducks.

Toward the end of the day I waded the shore line to get into the high hill behind us and have a look-see. Hundreds of mallards got up from the smaller rice bed when I came too close, and one of these, choosing the hill course, was tumbled with a thump to the soggy, acorn-strewn growth on the hilltop. It felt good to pick one out like that. Too bad the President didn't see it, in view of the performance he had witnessed from my pickle barrel.

The others milled over the rice, against a dark, wet, ragged sky. It was a wild and lovely moment—even lovelier when speedsters running the blockade at the blind came in range and I heard the deliberately spaced booms of the President's automatic.

Back in the oaks over the high hill there was less rain and wind. The forest floor underfoot was a silent carpet of yellow and bronze. A man can often flush a deer in there after the acorns have fallen. I saw one, a furtive doe quietly slipping away. She never dreamed she was seen. Snowshoe rabbits were already changed from brown to white. I walked back with my lone duck.

"Only one?" snorted Mister President. "I saw a million get out of there—well, two hundred, anyway. That's more'n a million."

"He was the only one that came in range."

Mister President pointed to his own comfortable pile, close to a limit. Just as I was about to insert myself in the pickle barrel my eye caught a piece of shell-box cardboard. The President had stuck it on the rim of the barrel and had written thereon: "TO LET—One smelly old pickle barrel. Only good duck shots need apply. Owner going out of business. Chance for a good man to build up thriving trade."

After the laughter had been swallowed up in the tamaracks and I had missed another bird and the President had declared a halt—"for fear you'll get the habit permanently"—we picked up and headed for the car. Nosing out of the sand trails through the dripping woods, I acknowledged his master-minding anent the little flight.

"But," I insisted, "I can't figure out why I couldn't hit 'em. You suppose that pickle barrel had anything to do with it?"

He snorted and half turned beside me to deliver his dictum with full impact: "Boy, your shooting and that pickle barrel both smell the same to me."

*Some things change. Others do not. Some
things of life remain timeless because the
enduring human values are relatively static, if
indeed they have changed at all.*

*It is not generally considered that automobiles
fall into the unchangeable category. It should
therefore come as a surprise that the original
star of this story was a Model T Ford built in
1921. Since this vintage vehicle has now achieved
a classic antique status, use of its name carries a
meaning MacQuarrie did not intend and the
name Jeep—a venerable vehicle with no status as
yet—has been substituted for the Model T.
Except for editing away a few mechanical
differences, that is the only change. All else
remains the same . . . and timeless.*

*Since automobiles obviously do change, the
enduring element here is the enthusiasm for, and
the use of, a hunting and fishing vehicle.
Probably a couple of Egyptians stood in the
shadows of the rising pyramids and chortled
over a beat-up chariot, acquired solely for
hunting and fishing. The only reason we can't
enjoy it with them is that MacQuarrie
wasn't there.*

12

The Ultimate Automobile

From time to time, inspired almost solely by the President of the Old Duck Hunters' Association, Inc., I have set forth the code and standards of this two-man fraternity as they relate to trout fishing, duck hunting, and the best time to trade in a shotgun.

For a number of years I have tried to outline the creed and the methods of the Association, which are in fact the creed and methods of the President of the Old Duck Hunters himself, the same being an aging man with graying hair and a bang-up set of hundred-year-old duck decoys.

I have reported faithfully about the ancient brown mackinaw which he wears in frigid duck blinds, of the patched rubber-bottom packs in which he cruises the deer woods, and of the little crooked pipe wherein he burns tobacco and creates gurgles. I have also told of those moments when human frailty overcame him and he rested on the oars when it was his turn to pull. He can hike when he has to.

I have told how he loathes to put on the storm windows when the bluebills are flying, and of how he maintains an angleworm ranch in his back yard as a form of trout stream insurance. I have even told, with proper modesty I hope, of his dear wife, Missus President, whom he thinks he has been fooling these many years, and how she sometimes grins to herself and mutters, "the old fool. . . ."

Anent these things I have tried to be a faithful reporter,

often abashed at the task, for Hizzoner, Mister President, is
no man to be pinned on cork and examined like a dead
butterfly. Though he is but one person, and a good and
salty one, he is also a symbol of outdoorsmen, representing
the one and only old-timer of the woods and waters. Where
would we fingerlings be without his kind?

Also at times when the Old Man has prodded me to it I
have hinted at his vocational pursuit, which happens to be
automobiles new or used. To this commercial eminence he
arose via a seasoning as tailor's apprentice, Great Lakes sailor,
timber cruiser, carriage painter, candy salesman, civic leader—
and a hell of a good judge of how a new corncob pipe will
break in.

Sometimes, merely in passing, intent upon outdoor trans-
actions of an immediate nature, I have mentioned that the
vehicles we use in getting about country have usually been
certain ancient jalopies plucked from the half-acre used car
lot he owns. This is a place he seems to prefer to the shining
showroom with its bright new cars.

It may seem removed from the outdoor game to qualify
Mister President as a topnotch trout fisherman by pointing
out that he can size up a used car merely by walking around
it and kicking its tires. Yet I suspect that the same insight
which guides him to the best mallard pothole opening day
is closely akin to the perception he displays in studying out
the good and the bad on a new trout stream.

He simply walks around those worn-out phaetons kicking
the tires. He never lifts the hood, or pretends in any way to
vast mechanical knowledge. He walks around 'em, kicks the
tires and says "A hundred and fifty even," and the deal is
made. Could it be?—I think it is so—that this same kind of
savvy leads him in November with unerring instinct to the
stand where the buck will sneak out from cover and make a
try for it across the burn?

Almost always we of the Association have gone to the

places of the fish and the fowl in one of Mister President's temporary automotive headaches. Almost always we have come back in them. Sometimes he has had to try hard to remember what the "Owner's Handbook" for a given model said to do when the carburetor flooded. Often we have propped up these horseless carriages for a tire change, with jacks or with pry poles cut from nearby spruce swamps. Once we persuaded an old goat of a car to lurch up a muddy hill with nothing more than our woollen socks wrapped around the wheels in lieu of chains.

Oh my, but the Old Duck Hunters has had experience with man's best friend, the automobile. Occasionally when Hizzoner was not satisfied with the sound his toe made against a tire, we have ushered spic and span $2,000 jobs down scratchy roads where a mule would hate to go. Once, in a conveyance with faulty brakes which took fire, we extinguished the flames to the rear with a couple hatfuls of ditch water.

Always it has been that the best of the fishing and hunting days came when Mister President selected some time-worn klunk that did not seem to mind if we tossed wet waders into it. Those shiny equipages somehow look out of place in the back country where the Association carries on the rites. In fact, farmers in whose yards we often park are inclined to doubt our integrity if we come around in anything valued at more than $150, on the hoof.

Mister President once upon a time decided to appropriate a permanent hunting and fishing car. I watched him size up the used jobs that came along. He tested their heaters to make sure they would dry out wool socks on a cold day. And of course he walked around them kicking their rubber, like a spaniel pup walks around his first pheasant.

He ruled out the big ones. He calculated that inasmuch as I weigh no more than 160 in wet waders we had ought to get something light enough to h'ist out of mudholes. He avoided the middle-sized ones because he said their owners pushed them too fast trying to keep up with the big ones. He settled upon a creation known far and wide as the Jeep. He phoned me the evening he closed the deal.

"Feller from the country had it," he explained. "He said his wife demanded something better and he'd done pretty well on clover seed last year."

"I understand his wife's feelings," I said, surveying the car.

"Isn't she a honey?" said Mister President. "Thirty-two fifty I allowed him but I could have bought it for $10 cash."

The car was vintage Detroit, born with its thousands of litter mates at a time when autos knew not whether to come out with smooth-treaded tires, or whether they should burst forth clad in the grandeur of those great big four-inch cleats. The erstwhile owner had plumped for the smooth little tires. Mister President could make them thump like a bass drum on a hot day when he kicked them, although at each kick I expected something to give.

"How's the motor?"

"It goes."

"And the brakes?"

"Just relined," he said.

"And the coils, and the head gasket, and the water pump, if any, and the front bushings?"

The President of the old Duck Hunters shot at me: "You'd be a hell of a man to put in charge of the used car lot."

The old speedometer on the dash was covered with the dust and grease of the years. I rubbed some of it off and read the dial—74,000 miles. It had possibly ceased to function 10 years previous. It was a station wagon, so-called, with a ragged roof.

"Nothing to that," said Mister President. "If the roof leaks we can tar and gravel it."

In a matter of days he phoned to announce that he had

filled the nine gallon tank beneath the seat, had pumped up the tires, and would travel with me to the St. Croix River of north Wisconsin if I could be ready at 4 P.M.—no later. I was ready.

He chugged up to my curb, came to a chattering halt and got a pailful of water which he poured down the creature's throat. Then he got in behind the wheel. There was something about that ensemble that was perfect. The rim of his brown hat came down over his eyes at the identical angle made by the ragged top of the puddle jumper.

This was his "permanent hunting and fishing car" and he was proud of his transaction, so I did not offer to drive. He raced the motor. Reverberating explosions sounded from somewhere beneath us. "Just listen to that power," he said.

We surged out of the neighborhood with the shattered muffler lying in the street and wondering neighbors leaning on their lawn mowers obviously saying to themselves, "Heaven help us, where'd he get THAT?"

"Not a bad riding job, eh?" he said as we jounced south on a gravel road.

"Not bad," I agreed, but unable to resist, "How's your bridge work?"

"These are the cars," he said. "These new-fangled machines are made for people without spines. I'll take an old crate like this every time."

At a country filling station we drew up and laved the Jeep's interior with oil.

"Not bad," he said, getting back in. "She used only two quarts in 30 miles!"

"We could get a tinner to make an oil pan to catch what she throws out and pour it back in," I suggested.

"My boy," said Mister President, "you are riding in the grandest mechanical contrivance in history for fishermen. This is a man's car, the first and final word in the efforts of the Society of Automobile Engineers to build transportation for folks who want transportation. We never took a better car off the lot."

He paused, his arms jolting against the loose steering wheel, and pronounced: "This is the Ultimate Automobile!"

"I hope she doesn't explode or disintegrate or collapse."

"Faw!" he said, pressing down the accelerator four more notches.

Driving along, often sidewise on the corduroyed gravel, the way a dog runs when he's idling home, he enlarged upon his philosophy of cars and fishing and people.

"I like old things," he said. "I like old sweater jackets and old hitching posts. I like old ivy vines climbing up a wall and old friends."

It was certainly true. Well able to afford newer things, the Old Man clung nostalgically to older items. The Jeep was one of the items. That he was dearly in love with it was plain as anything from the way he clung to the wheel when she hit a hole in the road, and how he exulted when the mechanism under the hood triumphed over hills.

The place where we hit the St. Croix is reached to the east from U. S. Highway 35, via County Trunk Highway T. The stream is bridged here. If you are careful and not going too fast, you will find a fair parking place on the east side of the bridge, but look out for niggerhead rocks which lurk in the grass. Mister President's Ultimate Automobile came to a shuddering halt and pretty soon we were out there on the river, one of the best of the smallmouth streams in the entire Middle West.

I like to wade it upstream here, remaining within fly line distance of the banks. In high water it is best not to try to wade this water at all. The season was July, so we had no trouble. He went off down stream in his patched waders with the husky fly rod with the 14-inch-long cork grip.

It was a good evening. I stood off from the left bank of the St. Croix and dropped yellow feather minnows in likely places, especially at the edges of holes such as are covered at their tail ends with river-borne logs and leaves.

This is not at all like trout fishing. Personally I do not believe it is as good as trout fishing, but then when a two-pound smallmouth makes up its mind I don't argue needlessly. I try to set the hook and take the rascal away from the snaggy hole. Then the fish rushes out into the current and yanks at me, seeming to say "So you think trout have got something, just take a look at this!"

It was a good evening indeed. I worked the feather minnow at a right angle across the current trying for the bank fish that come out so viciously. By dark I was up quite a ways from the iron bridge.

An old bog pumper began working his kitchen pump. A flock of swallows got after their evening meal over the broad river. The high, round hills of the St. Croix valley stood out in silhouette to the west. I walked back to the rendezvous in knee-deep July, with the first faint night mist curling up into warm air from the cool river.

There was the old crate, pretty lop-sided looking, but an appropriate companion to the President of the Old Duck Hunters, who sat on the running board with a sandwich and a cup of thermos coffee. We munched and talked. He had shown the downstream smallmouths standard wet flies, bass size with spinner. He had enough bass in his creel to make several neighbors happy. Finished, I asked him if he thought the old Jeep would start.

"Haw," he said. "Start? She can't help but start. She's been doing nothing else for 18 years!" He gave it a pat or two, walking around kicking the tires.

"I'm going to trick this old girl out," he said. "I'm going to make a lady out of this Tin Lizzie. She's just the car we need in our business."

He warmed to the subject—

"I'm going to put on brand new tires. I'm going to paint

'er a drab olive so we can use 'er for a duck blind if we have
to. Look at the clearance, a good 16 inches. When you
throw 'er into low she'll drag through anything.

"I've got four chrome tanned buckskins in the attic. I'll
get an upholsterer to rip off all the stuff inside and put in
the buckskin—she'll be a sporty looking job, and rugged too.

"Then I'll get Roy at the garage to rebore the block, put
in a new carburetor and along the ceiling inside we can rig
up some hooks for holding casting rods.

"I'll build a hell of a big plywood trunk and hang it on
the back, put in a trailer hitch and then we can drag a duck
skiff anywhere. Comes winter and we'll put on chains and
leave them on. We'll take that car any place. Might even
build up the front springs with two or three extra leaves to
keep 'er from lurching."

He walked around the car kicking the tires. He peered
underneath it, vastly pleased with how high the battery was
off the ground.

"For next to nothing," he opined, "I can make a new car
out of 'er."

We stowed away gear.

"When we get that trunk built on we can put all our
tackle in the back there," he said. "Why, we can just toss
our stuff in that trunk in May and leave it there until
October!"

He stepped on the starter. From down in the basement
of the car came a dull grinding. He stepped on the starter
again and again—and yet again. "Well," he said, "that's
nothing. Just a minor problem."

He checked and I checked. He found the gas supply sufficient. He determined that the connections for ignition were
apparently sound. He banged the rickety old hood up and
down a score of times. The spark plugs came out one by
one. He found the timer and removed it and cleaned it. He
tested the coil.

"Might be," he said, "that the valves are sticking."

"Might be," I said, "a splendid idea to set fire to it and forget it."

"Destroy a perfectly good automobile? Wait until I get 'er in shape. She'll be like new!"

We went over everything again and interminably. We flooded 'er and unflooded 'er. In the process the right rear tire sighed suddenly and gave up the ghost. The Jeep after 18 wearing years, was collapsing all at once, like the one-hoss chaise.

The moon came out and rode high through a sea of clouds above the lovely St. Croix valley. It was near midnight when I persuaded him to abandon ship. We waited on the iron bridge and were lucky to catch a ride to town on a belated pulp wood truck, the driver of which had been out visiting his girl. It was several days after that I made contact again with Mister President. He explained all.

"Next day I sent Roy down with the wrecker to pick 'er up. By gosh, she was gone! Somebody swiped our car. Roy couldn't find any tracks other than that Jeep's own tracks. He thinks the thief got 'er to going with a hairpin in the ignition keyhole."

So there went glimmering the Old Duck Hunters' opportunity to own a home of its own. Somewhere no doubt, coursing through the jack pine and scrub oak of north Wisconsin, is our Jeep, running when it chooses, standing bravely to its task of serving mankind.

Since then, the Association has reverted to the use of the handiest used car available on the Old Man's lot. One day not long after a promising-looking model of the same lineage landed on Mister President's lot. It really looked pretty good, but when I asked him if he intended to admit it to full membership in the Association, he snorted.

"A Wagoneer for the Old Duck Hunters' Association? Too darned modern. Wait 'til they've proven themselves!"

MacQuarrie didn't invent the moral of this tale —that to receive something worthwhile, you've got to give plenty. And he makes little of it in consequence.

What is more interesting and much more unique here, is the fun he has telling it. It is a rare, rare writer who communicates the feeling that he is enjoying the story as much as you are. I defy anyone to say MacQuarrie isn't getting a boot out of the trout that race across his typewriter and, in this case, isn't excited by the big-hooked buck sneaking down the page.

A writer's task is different from most in that he is forced to play God. He punishes the wicked, rewards the virtuous or vice versa as he sees fit. His thoughts about people and things, deeply felt, often are arrived at only in torment. MacQuarrie had his demons like all men. Vanquished them, too.

As a writer he had to worry whether his words conveyed what he actually felt. Whether the great emotions or exhilarations of one heart could, in fact, be transferred to another via the same shop-worn words that describe kitchen cleansers and carburetor adjustment. Each sentence is a worry. Each paragraph. Each page.

So when it comes out fun, you think the guy who put this down was a good guy and is having a ball, make no mistake . . . It wasn't an accident. It didn't just happen. It's called mastery. And it doesn't happen very often.

13

You've Got to Suffer!

The President of the Old Duck Hunters' Association, Inc., was waiting for me; so I had to get in there, even if the snow was a foot deep on the level and heavily drifted. I lay on my back in city clothes to jack up the rear wheels for tire chains, wishing that the guy who had designed those petticoat fenders was properly punished for his sins against a humanity which at some time or other simply must use auto chains.

The chains, momentum and good luck took me into a solid three-foot drift. Well, I got halfway through it. A half hour of shoveling ensued, and then I turned off the back road on the narrow, twisting by-road.

It was a shambles of drooping pine trees. Jack-pines thirty feet tall and up to five inches thick were arched over the road, weighted down under tons of damp snow. A few clips with the pocket-ax which I always carried in the car snapped them; then it was necessary to shake the clinging snow from them and drag them off the road.

There would be no deer hunting the next day—I was sure of that. Getting about in that snow would be impossible. But I had said I would get in there. The Old Man was waiting. It is amazing what a man will do to keep a date with the President of the Old Duck Hunters.

I was six hours behind schedule when I stopped the car

beside Mister President's snow-shrouded car. I was sweating and unsteady afoot. There had been almost a whole day of nerve-racking driving in the storm before the final climactic effort to get over that last half mile. I grabbed pack-sack and rifle and wallowed to the door of the place.

The Old Man was asleep, with his feet stretched toward the fireplace. I moved quietly. I put new wood on his fire, broke out duffle and had the teakettle going in the kitchen before he awoke. He called from the big room, "That you, Tom?"

"Yep," I answered, sounding as much like Tom as I could.

"When did you get here?"

"Minute ago."

Tom is a neighbor who is likely to appear at the abode of the Old Duck Hunters almost any time. The Old Man continued, still unsuspecting:

"Where do you suppose that whelp of a boy is? Said he'd be here for supper, and it's midnight."

I heard him yawn and heard him wind his watch. Then he said: "Dammit, Tom, I'm worried. He might try to make it here in this storm, and he doesn't know the first thing about driving a car in snow."

"And never will. Don't worry about him. He'll hole up in some luxurious hotel down the line and wait for the snow-plows."

That speech was too long. The Old Man's feet hit the floor, and he stamped to the kitchen, all sympathy vanished.

"You pup of a boy!" he snorted. "You lame-brained rooster!" He carried on over a snack of tea and toast. "Cars stuck all over the country. This is the worst storm ever hit this country before a deer season opening."

I looked around. He had brought in enough wood to last for several days. I said, "We'll just hole up, as long as we can't hunt."

"Not hunt!"

He had it all figured out. He'd looked over the near-by thoroughfare country in the storm and had found deer working down into it, out of the more open jack-pine on higher ground.

"We'll hunt, all right!"

That was the last thing I heard before dropping off to sleep. I think I did not change my position once, and slept until noon, right around the clock.

"I'm saving you," he explained. "Had to get you in shape. You're going to make one little drive to me."

"I'm not mooching in this snow."

The Old Man pointed to the wall at the end of the room. "See those snowshoes? All you've done to them the last two years is varnish 'em. Today you're going to wear off some varnish."

It was bitter cold, near zero, after the snow had ceased and the clouds passed. All right, if the Old Man was going to sit on a stump in that weather, he was going to put on some clothing. I persuaded him, over his objections, to pile on plenty of underwear, a wool sweatshirt and a heavy outer shirt. He bulged rather ridiculously, I had to admit, with all that clothing, but for good measure I made him carry along my huge, ungainly but wonderfully warm sheep-lined aviation boots.

He hated the clothes that bore him down. I knew what he wanted to wear—just his regular duck or deer-season gear, which is not too much, topped off with the old brown mackinaw. He vowed that the only way a man could wait out a deer was to do a little personal freezing.

I had to laugh when he started out. He was so swaddled in clothes that he could hardly turn his neck above the shawl collar of the ancient mackinaw. But I did not laugh, for I was afraid he'd go back into the house and shed some of the garments, and in that searching cold I could not see him suffering while I took what is really the easier course, moving and so keeping warm.

South of us lay the Norway pine hill facing the thoroughfare, or river, between two lakes. Mister President had it all figured out. He would take an old stand at the top of the Norway hill. I would circle to the south and west of him, then drive up through the thick cover lying at the edge of the thoroughfare. If anything with horns came through, he would have shooting as it hit the open Norway grove.

Northwest Wisconsin, in twenty years, never saw a storm like that one at that season. Nor did it, in that time, see cold like that so early, combined with deep snow. The freak storm kept hundreds out of the bush. It was the first day of the four-day buck season. We had the country practically to ourselves. Most of the army of hunters was waiting for the snow to settle or thaw. And a four-day doe season was coming up in seven days.

Mister President's self-imposed assignment was to mush through the snow for about a mile, hard going without snowshoes, which he does not like. I left him plodding through the stuff toward his stand and began the great circle which would bring me below him.

At any rate, that snow was good for snowshoeing. It had the solid permanence of snow that has lain and settled and proposes to stay until spring—which it most certainly did.

It felt good to be on snowshoes again, carrying a rifle. I went through a long pulpwood slashing. All the tracks in that slashing confirmed what Mister President had said—that deer were moving into the denser cover, away from the open pinelands. Down there along the thoroughfare's edge they could find protection and browse, even some white cedar—champion of all winter deer browse.

The slashing was lovely. A bluejay yammered at me. Chickadees hung upside down on branches. Will someone tell me how these minute wisps of down maintain their high spirits in the face of any weather? A red squirrel in a jack-pine cussed me roundly: "Bad enough for this storm to come so early without you moving in on my property!"

Snow-bent jacks lopped to the southwest, for the snow had come from the northeast, off Lake Superior. That storm gave the North a wonderful pruning. Old Lady Nature every so often throws one like that over her wild garden to nip off old branches, weed out the weak ones and compel the strong ones to prove it.

There was plenty of snow down my neck. Charlie Garvey, the forest ranger at Gordon, had warned me the evening before: "Stuff is down so much the rabbits can't get through." He knew, too, that the impact of this storm had pushed vast supplies of browse within reach of hungry deer. Incidentally, before winter was finished in the North, the sly dame did the same thing on two more occasions. So that deer got plenty to eat and the forests had a splendid pruning.

When I got to the thoroughfare where I was to turn back and drive north, I sat down a minute. At this place the thoroughfare drops three feet. There were wings overhead, belated bluebills and early golden-eyes hunting water in the frozen lake country.

The sun was varnishing the jack-pine tops as I began the drive. In the shadows the snow was turning lavender. Downy and hairy woodpeckers hid behind tree trunks as I went along. The snowshoes creaked. I followed the thoroughfare edge. There was ice out from shore forty yards at my right. At my left and ahead of me was thick cover.

There were many tracks, all old ones. Deer had certainly come down here out of the pinelands in the night. But where were they now? Then I saw a fresh track. You know how it is—that virgin white scar of a hoof in snow, so unlike the settled, stiffened track of twelve hours before.

The deer was moving ahead of me. Buck or doe? I do

not know. Even in fresh mud I do not know, and I think that no one else can tell for certain. That track was big and brand-new. It was a mark left by a critter moving exactly the way the Old Duck Hunters wanted it to move—straight north toward the Old Man.

This deer was not plunging. It seemed to know my pace and kept just ahead of me. Likely it had heard me when I was a hundred yards away from it, had got up quietly and just sneaked away from me. You wonder at such times where the rascals get the wisdom to know that a man in snow cannot move rapidly. Deer can be very contemptuous of a man.

The wind was not a factor. There was a little drift from the northwest. Up in the open slashings it could be felt. Down along the thoroughfare bottoms, however, pipe smoke went straight up.

Sometimes this deer stayed on the beaten trails which had been worked in the night before. Sometimes it cut across lots through fresh snow. Contemptuous of me? Indeed, and then some.

I saw where, during the night of the storm, deer had come into the thoroughfare bottoms and nibbled on cedar. Even the little fellows could live off a storm like that. Everything was caved in, trees formed solid white wigwams, branches drooped—as inviting a deer cafeteria as you might wish to see.

Why hadn't this big one moved out of the bottoms with the others? Was it an old grandfather or a grandmother that chose the easy living of this place to getting out of there and seeing country? Once I thought I saw it a hundred yards ahead, but that turned out to be mere flipping of white snow from a branch released from pressure—not a flag.

My deer had passed the place where the snow slid off the tree, a full twenty yards to the west. A calculating beggar, that animal. Just so far ahead of me—no farther.

Well, if a buck, it was venison on the pole. It went dead

on toward a rendezvous with a .30-30 carbine held by a very steady old gentleman in an old brown mackinaw.

That critter had me figured out so well that sometimes it even stopped to browse. It would pay for that—if it was what Mister President called "a rooster deer." Contempt of court, that's what it was! Just wait until that old goat moved out from the thick stuff and started ambling through those open Norways! The Old Man has killed a half dozen bucks from that stand. Most of them have dropped within an area not larger than a baseball diamond.

Good, I thought. Whatever it was, it was right on the beam going in. The darkness drew down. Purple worked up to the zenith from the eastern sky. I moved that deer along the way a farm collie brings home the cows. Finally I saw him.

He was across an opening, perhaps a hundred yards off. He was big and dim. No question now what he was. He was "he." His rack went up and back like branches on an old oak. I might have had one quick fling at him, but why chance it? The Old Man was waiting, and it was better to move that deer into the open Norway grove. Then, if the first one didn't clip him, there would be other chances.

I went along. I know that terrain as well as the buck knew it—almost as well as the Old Man knows it. Pretty soon, up ahead, there would be a shot. Just one shot, it ought to be. That would be the Old Man's 150 grains of lead and copper going to its destination. Then silence—the sort of quiet after one shot that means so much to a deer hunter.

It was working out perfectly. In my mind's eye I pictured the Old Man, alert on his hillside. I saw him scan the cover, saw the buck walk out and turn to listen along its back trail. I saw Mister President draw down on the buck, wait until the buck stood with cupped ears, raise the little rifle and squeeze it off. Yes, I even pictured him setting down the rifle and reaching for the big, bone-handled clasp-knife in his right hip pocket.

It was as easy as falling off a log. Mister President's formula had been right. If the ground had been bare, that buck might have busted through the Norway grove with his foot to the floorboard.

I wondered if we should drag him the mile home. Or if we should borrow Hank's toboggan, or just commandeer his truck, which has high wheels and is at home in deep snow. I decided that with the weather cold as it was we could dress him, hang him, cool him and have decent steaks by supper-time tomorrow.

Minutes passed. The Old Man would let him have it now. . . . Or now. . . . Now, then! The buck must be in the Norways at the foot of the hillside. Heavens above, he must be halfway up the hillside! I could see the big Norways ahead of me. The only sound was the creak of the snow-shoes and the "kra-a-a-ak" of a raven.

I broke through the bottomland cover and faced the hill-side. Over the hilltop in back of the old man I saw the buck the second time, slowly and contemptuously effacing him-self from me.

I took one quick shot. It was just a shot at a skulking shadow, and I knew as I pulled the trigger in the instant I had for shooting that I was over him a good two or three feet.

At the shot Mister President waved to me from his stand. I trudged up the hill to him. He looked guilty.

"You git 'im?"

"Mister President, do not speak to me ever again."

He made a clean breast of it, then and there. "All right, I fell asleep. Your shot woke me."

It was plain as sin what had happened. Mister President had brushed the snow off a fallen Norway and sat there a while. He had lit a fire. He had banked browse against that two-foot-thick down log so that he could stretch out. Then

—oh, my brethren!—he had fallen asleep. "Dammit, I had too many clothes on," he said.

And then I just had to laugh. He wasn't the Mister President of other deer drives, chilled and lean and ready, with a drop on the end of his nose. He was swathed and cluttered sleep-producing items—those huge aviator's boots, which are with clothes, and over his swampers he had drawn the final, comparable to separate steam-heating systems.

We went home, boiled the kettle, and ate pork chops and boiled potatoes. We drank quarts of tea. At bedtime the Old Man announced: "If anyone tries to tell me what to wear tomorrow, I will resign the presidency of the Old Duck Hunters. I must have dozed there for two hours."

The next day we did it again. The weather had moderated. He went to the same stand. I made the long swing south and west on the snowshoes and drove up through the thoroughfare bottoms. Making the drive, I knew that now the Old Man was standing there by his down log, in his thin swampers, I knew that sometimes he shivered, and sometimes he whapped his arms across his breast to get circulation going. I knew that he'd move up and down on his feet and wriggle his toes, and that he was standing there with his earlaps up, so that he could hear better.

The drive was easy. There were more deer in the bottoms along the thoroughfare. Driving up through and watching the tracks ahead of me, I felt that I was pushing a whole herd into that Norway grove. One of them might be Old Horny, might be the same old fellow who beat the Old Duck Hunters yesterday, hands down.

Pow! He had shot just once. I came into the grove at the foot of the hillside, and Mister President called down to me: "He's lying over to your left. Four hens came out, and the rooster after them."

I do not know whether it was the same buck. I think it was another. The one of the day before seemed a larger animal. There he was, a good ten-pointer. I called up the hill: "Bring your knife down here, and I'll dress him out."

He came sliding down the hill in the snow. "I'll dress him out myself. Maybe I can get warmed up that way."

Mister President was certainly a sight. His nose was red and his lips were blue. He was hunched and shivering beneath the old brown mackinaw. The wait in the cold had been a long one, but worth it. He went to work, and I went off to fetch Hank with his truck. When we got back, the Old Man had finished the job—had even dragged the buck up his hillside and out to the road to meet the truck.

"Well, you sure got warmed up," I said.

"I did," he agreed. "But you got to suffer first."

There isn't any question that the high jinks between the junior and senior member of the ODHA, Inc. sustained the popularity of the yarns. In Backache Bass *you will find some of the highest jinks of all. MacQuarrie was usually a gentle humorist, but he could march gladly into a slapstick situation when the occasion arose.*

14

And like any God-fearing man he could, if called upon, even amid the horseplay step into the pulpit and preach a bit:

"What adventures we miss by not going off the path a bit, and how easy it is to get just a little way beyond where the other fellow stops. And how easy, too, to find things in our own back yards that most other fishermen do not know are there."

It doesn't detract from the fun at all. Far from it.

Backache Bass

The President of the Old Duck Hunters' Association, Inc., wasn't going fishing. He had told me Saturday that he had reformed and was going to work in his yard all day Sunday. I got up early Sunday and prowled the neighborhood. From across the street, where I chatted with a lawn-mowing neighbor, I saw Mr. President on his knees transplanting things out of little brown pots. His wife stood guard.

We spoke no greeting, but watched each other secretly. The President had put on his faded old fishing jacket and battered hat with its fly-studded rim. He would transplant two or three of the potted herbs, and then take off that old felt hat and study the flies. Then he'd replace the hat and reach resolutely for another little brown pot.

After a while he relit his dead cigar and stared at me. It wasn't long before he was glaring at me.

I said nothing. I discussed baseball with the lawn-mowing neighbor who rattled off batting averages above the clatter of the blades. When the mower's voice dwindled, I could hear piteous sighs escaping from Mr. President. Once I heard him mutter sadly, "Man may work from sun to sun, but woman's work is never done."

By this time, Mrs. President had walked around to the front of her house and was examining the shrubs. The President darted a quick glance in her direction and suddenly hurried through the back door. In a moment he reappeared and shouted across to me: "Someone wants to talk to you on the telephone. They must have thought you'd be loafing around here."

I crossed the street and entered his house. He followed me inside. The phone on the breakfast-room table had its

161

receiver in place. I asked if the party had left a number for me to call. Mr. President leaned on the gas range and sighed again. He was very sad—almost ill.

"If I go to hell," he said, "you gotta come along. You know I wanted to plant those danged tomatoes, or whatever they are. But like the snake in Eden, you got up early this morning to tempt me."

He flicked cigar ashes in the kitchen sink and continued. "I was driven from my bed at 6 A.M. Since then I've been working my fingers to the bone while you've been standing across the street in your store clothes doing nothing. Can't you see that if I don't get this job done it's gonna be too late?" There was despair in his voice now.

"Too late for what?"

"To fish the Eau Claire Lakes."

"I thought you'd reformed."

"I had until you came along to tempt me. You ought to know better than come nosing around when I'm on the straight-and-narrow."

"Yeah. I saw you with that jacket on—and gazing at those flies."

"Well"—apologetically, when he saw I wouldn't accept the blame—"you know how it is."

"Oh."

"When I get through with the transplanting, it appears the wife is going to put me to work digging out dandelions on a share-cropper's basis. But if you'd just run along home, get into your Sunday clothes and come running back with a rod and tackle box, I might get away. My wife is a very kind person. . . ."

I did it—sauntered back home, wondering if Mrs. President had seen the conclave held in her kitchen, and in twenty-five minutes hurried back. Mr. President was very busy tamping the dirt around the last one of the little plants.

"I've been planting this one for ten minutes," he hissed.

"Why didn't you hurry? If she'd got me started on those dandelions, there'd have been no hope. Now do your stuff."

I strove manfully to make it appear a matter of course that he would come with me. I even lied. I said I wanted to see a man about a boat, which was pretty good offhand stuff, even though only a variation of seeing a man about a dog. Mrs. President heard, came, pondered.

The President, on his knees in a supplicating attitude, cast his eyes to the ground and sorrowfully said he couldn't come. I said I was going alone and started back toward my car, which was parked across the street. I heard the rascal sigh. Had I been as close as his wife, I might even have seen a tear cascade off his nose into the brown earth as his poor, tired fingers tucked soil about the last plant.

Just as I reached the curb Mrs. President up and said: "Quit squeezing the earth around that plant! You'll squeeze it to death." Then, eying him sharply: "Oh, go on, you old fool—and don't think either of you kidded anyone!"

He leaped up and tore around the corner of the house on two wheels. Almost instantly he returned with a fresh cigar emitting fire and smoke, brown eyes alight with fishing fever, his arms cluttered with rods, nets, boots. He was in a hurry until his wife said he needn't be, because she wasn't going to change her mind.

And that's how we got away. Thirty miles from home, at Brule, Wisconsin, I turned the car on to the velvet sand roads and we threaded south over the jack-pine hillocks. Now, I know those Eau Claire Lakes. I know them as well as you know the inside of your garage. I've seen northern lakes all the way from Watersmeet, Michigan, west to the Canadian boundary lakes of Minnesota. I've sat in duck blinds and rowed boats over too many lakes, but none of them have hit me as have the Eau Claires.

I don't say they are the best fishing lakes. Offhand, I can think of a dozen better ones. I don't say they are the most beautiful—but they are almost. I say they are my favorite inland waters because the first time I ever caught a fish on a plug rod it was in the big Eau Claire.

I was twelve years old and stood on a sand spit and threw a pork rind into deep water. I knew how to throw it. I'd been practicing in my back yard with a spike tied to the line. The pork rind flashed out over that clear cold water, sank, was retrieved fast, according to the instructions on the little tin box it came in, and within twenty feet a six-pound northern had it.

I can see that baby yet. When I landed him, he seemed big enough to saddle. His jaws worked spasmodically. I found a rock and killed him. He was the first northern I had ever taken. He was beauty and fury incarnate. Do you wonder that I have reserved a special place in my heart for the Eau Claires?

We borrowed a steel rowboat from a friend. If I couldn't walk in and just take a boat without saying a word at half a dozen places on the Middle Eau Claire, I'd resign from membership in the brotherhood of man. We unscrewed the kicker because the President said he needed the exercise. But his back began to ache shortly after leaving the shore; so I got the exercise. He has a very handy back. One minute he's strong as a bull, breathing fury and defiance at every-one; the next, fairly writhing in pain from his lame back.

While I rowed, the President pawed over his fishing gear, untangled a plug rod and its accessories, and then leaned back with a grunt of satisfaction. He snapped to the leader an old yellow plug with a red head that had been in his kit for at least twenty years, one of a famous old name. I've wondered many times since if this old plug looks like a new one to the rising generations of fishes.

"Row me over to that bar off the point of your right," ordered the President, wincing with pain as he shifted his position to survey the lake.

I angled in toward the bar, surveying the bottom to get out just the right distance. He began shooting the wabbler in over good fish cover.

By that time, it was ten o'clock in the morning. Pan fishermen were flecking the lake here and there. The sun was hot on bare forearms. I yearned to seize a rod, but Mr. President, watching me carefully, gave diplomatic orders: "Inshore a little bit. Oops! Not too far. There! Now follow along the edge of this weed line—slowly."

Well, you can't let down a guy with a lame back.

A northern hit that battle-scarred wabbler after about twenty minutes of work. Mr. President knows how to make a northern do his stuff. He lets the fish see him. He reels it in on that first rush. You know how docilely they sometimes come. When he gets it close, he stands up in full view of the fish and moves the line from side to side.

To a northern, it's a green signal in traffic. Dumb kluck he is, but there's hidden power in that long body. Great leverage, too. If the darned fish only knew it, he could probably employ it to greater advantage than a bass in the same water with its much shorter length.

This one, about a four-pounder, took a frightened dive under the boat. He was at the surface one instant and under and on top of the water at the other side quicker than you can say "backache." The President, nimble as a squirrel, his back completely cured, maneuvered the line around the end of the boat and coaxed the northern closer again. The fish floated calmly four feet from the boat, until the rod tip was raised. Then he came to the top and let go like a broken clock spring. Another dive, deep this time, another coaxing pull to the top, and the President, standing up, shouted his applause as the fish thrust out his head and thrashed. I thought the fun had continued long enough and brought the fish in with a boat net.

"How's your backache?" I asked.

"My what? Oh!" Pain creased his face, and he sat down gingerly. You could almost hear the joints creaking again.

He took a couple more northerns, and then jollied me into rowing him out to a deeper reef, where he snagged a nice walleye with a deep-going plug.

We lunched under a gnarled white pine on a shelving sand bank, and the President recounted the story of the lakes thirty-five years ago when loggers were still winching rafts of white pine across their surfaces. He told of the 40-pound northerns, the heads of which I had seen in Bill Fletcher's boat-house; of Bill, long since dead and gone; of Joe Lynch and the smallmouths he and Joe used to take out of Bony Lake, one of the smaller Eau Claires. His mention of bass set me thinking; so when we resumed places in the boat—you know where I sat—I worked over to the place where the thoroughfare from this lake leaves on its one-mile trip to the Lower Lake. I wanted a crack at some smallmouths that I knew would be in that faster water.

To the President's amazement, I beached the boat. He said I couldn't quit on him—not with his back as sore as it was. He said, by gosh, it was a dirty trick. By that time I was in trout waders and had a brass rod rigged up. The President had an idea of his own.

"If you ain't strong enough to row," he said, "I'm gonna take the boat back to its rightful owner and go get me some trout. Over by Cable. Remember that creek the guys in the garage told us about a year ago? It's been in my mind since. No Man's Creek, he called it."

So it was agreed that he would row back, take my car, drive the thirty miles to the almost-forgotten creek, try for trout, then return by seven o'clock or thereabout and pick me up where a road crosses the thoroughfare which I was to fish.

This thoroughfare water of the Eau Claires' is as clear as gin. Where there isn't a top-water riffle you can count the pebbles six feet down. In all, there are about ten spots in this one-mile stretch of fairly fast water where small-mouths lurk. A project to improve this little river is now under way which will provide additional smallmouth cover. This thoroughfare and others linking the Eau Claires are not fished hard. Fishermen usually stick to their boats, passing up the better sport of the faster water.

A white bucktail that flattened on top of the water like part of grandpa's whiskers was offered. It turned up nothing until the second bend below the bridge, where I was to meet His Honor. There is a six-foot hole at the right bank. An underwater snag projects into the current. I let the bucktail float down unimpeded by the line (really a kind of dry-fly fishing downstream, but don't laugh). On the first try a dark bronze shoulder threw that gin-clear water aloft in a shower as a good one tried—and missed.

The bucktail was allowed to float dead beyond him, then retrieved carefully. Again it floated over his den, and again he dynamited up and out. He was a lumpy brown torpedo against the pure water he flailed. Again he missed.

I cast over him, and the bucktail, under water now, was jerked back minnow-fashion. I saw him come for it, saw him smash it and felt the rod throb to the handle as the hook was set. He made for the undercut bank, but I worked him out. He dogged it out in mid-current, and you can bet I was glad to embrace him in the net. No still-water small-mouth this, but a he-hellion of the fast places. His every move had telegraphed fight through the none-too-heavy bass rod.

I worked downstream, passing through a pine-bordered widespread reminding me of a certain duck day the autumn before, and below the ruin of an old lumber dam gate hooked another on the bucktail. This one, about a two-pounder, perhaps slightly smaller than the first, got mixed up in the roots of an old stump, but was worked away by easy pulling and a final chance-it-all jerk. You can't just strip in these chaps. There's power in their rushes and intelligence in their heads. This fellow took out unbelievable line and angled off across the current, where I let him tire himself out. What a satisfying weight are these thoroughfare bass as they come into the net, their red-rimmed eyes staring at you brazenly through the meshes!

I had enough bass, but took three or four smaller ones, which were put back. They were cagey that day, and showed signs of striking short.

It was nearing six o'clock, and I was a long way from the appointed rendezvous at the bridge. I worked back up in the lengthening shadows. Blue herons, kildeer and shitepokes got up before me, resentful of my intrusion as they came home to roost for the night in the thoroughfare. Floating muskrats eyed me suspiciously before camel-backing out of sight.

Any river is beautiful at the end of a day. I had the thoroughfare entirely to myself while other fishermen were on the lake in boats, wondering why they couldn't get the smallmouths to hit their plugs or flies. What adventure we anglers miss by not going off the path a bit, and how easy it is to get just a little way beyond where the other fellow stops! And how easy, too, to find things in our own back yards that most other fishermen do not know are there.

At the bridge I rested against the railing and listened to the three-mile current under the bridge. The President was on time. It was only a little after seven when he nosed the car down the little hill to the bridge and stopped. It was a good sign, for when Mr. President doesn't get his fish right off he usually stays until he does—regardless of who is waiting for him and where.

"How's your backache?"

He said it was very bad. He said he went to No Man's Creek over near Cable, got a farm boy to dig him worms, rigged up his telescopic rod and waded through a swamp to reach the creek. Once there, he explained, he'd catch three or four chubs in the creek—then wham! Brook trout! Sure enough, there they were in his creel, as pretty a mess of those dark-bodied, deep-woods brooks as anybody ever saw.

"But I can't see how you worked into that spot with your sore back."

"It's just my never-say-die spirit," he explained. "I don't know but what there's a curative power in that kind of water."

We went home, and Mr. President made his usual triumphant entry into the neighborhood, pointing out to all who gathered about his kitchen sink that it was he who caught the trout, not I—"and despite a very lame back—very lame indeed."

One year later I went with him to that town of Cable. And that time we both fished the Namakagon. I guess his back was sore or something. At any rate, for some reason he seemed to have found out something about No Man's Creek that bothered him. It didn't bother him very much, of course, being President of the Old Duck Hunters, but he was inclined not to talk about it and seemed very well satisfied with the Namakagon, although we got but few trout.

On the way home that night I drove into a filling station to load up with gas. I was concerned about No Man's Creek and asked the attendant if he knew anything about it. When I asked the question, the President started to cough violently. The attendant said it was a darned good creek. He said it was the best brush trout stream in Wisconsin, for his money.

"Hell, it ought to be," he concluded. "It's been privately owned and posted for the last four years!"

There isn't any accounting for these rapscallions. They gloriously defy analysis. What can you say about a man who takes something of yours, wears it out, then blithely offers it in trade for its replacement? You've got to love him or hate him. And when he is Mr. President, there isn't any doubt at all which you choose.

15

MacQuarrie was hitting his stride in the years that produced The Bandit of the Brule. *His stories were balanced and, of course, hilarious. He dwelt on the minor themes in which he took delight. The preference for old things to things that were new. Simple things. Natural things—the way a river looked, the smell of the earth, the heft of a grouse in hand; all expressed in Celtic lyricism.*

The halcyon years crowded out of his writing the brooding side of the man. But MacQuarrie, the mystic who laughs at men who try to bargain with the gods, knows the halcyon years can not last. His inner resources are gathering to deal with the inevitable when the time comes.

The Bandit
of the Brule

The President of the Old Duck Hunters' Association, Inc., was clinging to the lower pantry shelf, head and arms thrust into a top compartment where he stores fishing tackle. Ignoring my entrance, he got a new grip, shifted his feet and went on prodding a remote corner. From time to time he grunted and hoisted a foot, the better to stretch his five feet and seven inches. He made a desperate effort, almost slipped, and a Wedgewood saucer crashed to the floor. The President withdrew his head and said accusingly:

"Now you've done it!"

"Eh?"

"You pushed me. That's why I slipped. Wait until my wife finds out who broke that saucer!"

He glared at me. There is no use arguing with the President of the Old Duck Hunters' Association.

"Don't stand there gawping!" he snorted. "Get a broom—no! Don't throw the fragments in the waste basket. Hide them, you loon. My wife always looks in waste baskets!"

This remarkable man bounded from the shelf, dragging something with him. It was a pair of faded, patched fishing waders. He held them in the light from the window, pulled tentatively and something gave 'way at a seam.

"Now you've got me excited!" he shouted. "You've ruined a good pair of waders!"

171

No two square inches of those waders were without evidence of the vulcanizer's art.

"All right, I ruined your waders."

"How can a man fish without waders?"

I suggested he might buy another pair.

"Do you know what those waders cost?" he demanded truculently, and added before I could reply: "Thirty dollars. That's what they cost!"

I knew they cost $18.25 and said so.

"Not on your life. These were made to order. They had to send for 'em."

"Can't they send again?"

"Well, if you want to go to that expense it's all right with me . . . I want to be fair about it. I was going to take just whatever you had in stock. But if you really intend to duplicate these waders, the inseam measurement is—."

"Come to think of it I have an old pair."

"Old pair!" His manner was bristling. "As if I'd take an old pair. I'll take those your uncle sent you from Scotland. I know he was in jail when he sent them but I'm not particular."

That's how the President got my new waders. He stole across the street to my house and removed them while I mowed the lawn. I saw him sneaking back home with them, the dog tagging along behind. The dog was supposed to be my dog but had found a boon companion in Mister President. He seemed to have found advantages in the President's mode of life that I could not offer.

I was for going over to his house and stealing them back but my wife was against it. She said it served me right— "leaving things around where he can get his hands on them." There wasn't any use making a fuss. I'd have to get along that season as best I could with my hip-high rubber boots.

The President also had my fishing jacket and a box of my flies. I had received the flies as a Christmas present from him but he took them back the day after Christmas because he said I didn't appreciate such things. When I had demurred he turned on me:

"What did you give me for Christmas? Nothing but a little etching of a trout jumping. A fine spirit to show at Christmas! Grasping—that's what you are!"

The first day the President went fishing in my waders he repaired alone to a secret place—"you walk two miles through brush, wade a swamp and hit the stream. Take you there? So every Tom, Dick and Harry in town will find out about this place? Not much!" He returned at midnight and phoned me out of bed.

"Those darned waders you gave me," he commenced. "They're too long in the toes. You know I've got a short foot. When you buy waders it's a wonder you wouldn't think of someone besides yourself. When I get a sock on over them there's a big lump right in the toe. I never saw such da—."

"Then bring them back. They fit me."

"There you go—always grasping. What's more, there aren't any suspenders or suspender buttons on 'em—."

There was a weighty pause while he let that sink in; then his voice took on a cheerier note as he continued:

"But I fixed that. At first I held them up with one hand while I fished with the other. That was before I got the bright idea of slashing holes in the tops and rigging up suspenders out of a fly line—."

I had a sudden suspicion it was one of my fly lines. He confirmed it cheerfully:

"I took that old cream-colored double-tapered line I found in your fishing jacket and cut it up for suspenders. It worked pretty good. Next time you buy waders get some that don't need overhauling on the stream. Damif I ain't sick and tired of wasting good fishing time repairing your stuff!"

He hung up and I lay awake two hours wondering if I'd

left anything else lying around that he might have appropriated in his ingenuous fashion.

It was not until a week later, on the Cranberry River, that I fully realized how much those waders would cost me ere summer had fled. Returning at night to our parked car the President bade me pull off his and/or my waders. I always have to do that. I have tried for years to skid him along the ground but he anchors himself and I am very likely to fall over backwards myself.

"Them waders—," he began. "Cheap things. I just barely brushed against a spruce stub and rip! went the right leg. See? Just above the knee. But it's only a six-inch rip. You can get it vulcanized."

I did. It cost $2.40 for the job. It would have been cheaper if the tire shop man hadn't found three other weak spots and, like a dentist exploring for cavities, reinforced them.

Anyway, I got the waders back. But the President learned, somehow, that I had them repaired and crept into my house one night. That's how he got them back.

I did the best I could on the various trout waters of North Wisconsin in a pair of new tan rubber ducking boots. Good thing I had them. They always shipped water over the tops but they kept a fellow dry for a little while. Their rubber bottoms were slippery on the rocks but it was cheaper using them than risking a wife's disfavor by investing in new waders—"how much money have you spent on that junk already this year?"

Once more that season the President returned my waders for dry-docking. This restoration followed a trip he made up the north shore of Lake Superior with a worm-drowning crony by the name of Rudy. They always got brook trout back inland from the lake where the beaver had dammed the streams. Brooks up to a pound and a half. You go in there with the President or Rudy or you don't go at all. Naturally, hardly anyone but the President and Rudy go in there.

The waders looked pretty sick by that time. At the toes where he turned them up to fit his wading brogues, there were marked abrasions. They had been placed too close to a fire to dry out and as a result one leg had acquired a stiff, crepe-rubber appearance. But they still held out water. Especially after I had them re-vulcanized for an even three bucks. Even the tire shop man, who is an expert wader surgeon, shook his head by this time—"They're on their last legs," he said.

I thought sure I could retain them after that second vulcanizing. But the President, after letting a whole week slip by, braced me on a street corner and said in a voice that could be heard a half block away:

"It's a wonder you wouldn't return things that don't belong to you!"

Then he stalked away, leaving me to wonder what passers-by thought about me.

He got them that night, by stealth. Warning came too late when I heard him tramping back across the street, the dog following approvingly. He was whistling a jaunty air as I saw him pass under the street light on the corner, the waders folded under his arm.

A few days later a friend by the name of Tommy phoned to ask me if he might borrow my waders for a day. He said he knew a place. I told him he could have them if it was all right with Mister President. Through Tommy I learned later that the old rascal had invited him into his house with a bow, that he had produced potable liquid from a place in the basement.

Tommy said he laid the waders in the middle of the floor— "sure, Tommy, you can have 'em. Anything for a neighbor." Then they downed about four tumblers of what turned out to be chokecherry wine from the President's own trees. He said he forgot all about the waders and stayed up until 2 o'clock playing bridge.

Things went along like that as the season advanced. I followed the President faithfully to all the trout holes he knew—and he knows a lot of them. He tours about to these places on week-ends, not forgetting to drop in and say hello here and there. For instance, he says hello to the fellow who runs the portable sawmill on the banks of the Namakagon at Squaw Bend and to the fellow who is always waiting at dusk on Stone's bridge on the upper Brule.

I don't know who this last fellow is. It's too dark to see by the time we poke our canoe nose into the dock. But this fellow is always there. He leans over the bridge right near the dock and says "Howdy, boys." Maybe it's a different fellow every time but it sure looks like the same one there in the dusk, with the faint western sky outlining his droopy felt hat and folded arms. I don't think this fellow has any face at all. Anyway, I never saw it. The only part of him I ever saw are the khaki pants and heavy boots that are revealed in the little circle of light the President makes with a flashlight, showing him our catch.

Now when the season is about to close, when the northern maples are reddening and the popples show signs of yellowing, the President prepares for a solemn mission—the last day of the season. This is fully as important as the opening day. It involves a study of the almanac to determine when the sun rises, thus insuring an early start. It also involves an auto packed the night before, two alarm clocks, in case one doesn't work, and considerable prayer that the day will be fair, but not too fair; warm, but not too warm; cloudy, but not too cloudy.

He roused me long before there was a hint of gray in the east and led me, half asleep to his waiting chariot. There he bade me take the wheel while he crawled in among the duffle in the rear and went sound asleep after commanding: "McNeil's on the lower Brule."

So that was the place he had chosen . . . Good judgment,

I mused, as I wheeled through town, across the Nemadji river fill, under the ore dock approach where the laden cars thundered by overhead.

McNeil's . . . Not a bad place for the last day. The browns from Lake Superior have a habit of working upstream in late August. The President, with my now disreputable waders as a pillow, got in a solid two hours of sleep as I drove through the sweet August dawn. It was light when we drew up under the lone spruce in the clearing. River mist marked the pathway of the Brule along the valley as far as we could see. The President grumbled about the waders, put them on gingerly so as not to strain the seams, said he doubted if they'd last out the day, told me to be back at 11 for lunch and stalked off by himself downstream.

After he had departed I prepared myself for the final quest. I put on the inadequate rubber boots and wondered how long it would be before the water would come trickling over their tops. I never attempt to accoutre myself for the river while the President is messing around inside the car. He requires an acre lot in which to get ready. He goes through every jacket, bag, car pocket and corner and takes what suits his fancy, regardless of whose it is. I just sort of stand around hoping he won't see too much. When he is gone I dive in and take what's left.

The most magical place in the world for me at 5 o'clock in the morning on the last day of the trout season is the lower Brule of Wisconsin.

Then autumn has already laid a tentative finger on the country. The steep banks of the Bois Brule play hide and seek in the morning fog. The river is a sullen gray rope, more crooked than at any place on its 66-mile length. Water that was warm a month ago—yes, two weeks ago—seems suddenly frigid, the result of longer, colder nights.

It was a morning of mornings. Always, by some inscrutable legerdemain with the weather gods, the President arranges for perfect weather on final day. He admits he has a special arrangement with the people who prepare weather and will trade a good closing day for, say, rain on the day of the Odd Fellows' picnic.

Above this place we call McNeil's hole, there is a long stretch of fast water—perhaps 400 yards—with a two-foot sheer drop at the beginning of it. There I went and with a gold-bodied brown bivisible sought to solve the mystery of a plunk-plunk that sounded from the middle of a deep run. I'd have bet money that fish would have taken. Getting closer I saw him through the mist, a bold, two-pound brown, feeding steadily, coming clear out of water and plunking back.

No better time. Early morning and late evening are best for browns. They seem less wary then. Middle of the day tactics are not needed. I offered him the bivisible a score of times. I doubt if on any of the casts he saw the tell-tale leader or line. But he wouldn't come. He wouldn't come to anything I had. I did not put him down. I left him plunking there in the corrugated riffle—for what, I never learned.

Upstream a bit two smaller brownies surrendered to the lure of gold and two more came to net from flies dropped right into the churning froth beneath the little two-foot falls. I worked upstream. The sun was climbing. Mist evaporated. A porky swam the creek in front of me. By 11 o'clock, weary, hungry, I returned to the car.

The President had been there ahead of me. He had some fish. "Yes, I've got some good keepers—but them damn waders. Look at me! I'm soaking. I feel like a spaniel. Gimme a cup of coffee before I catch my death."

He dried out while we ate. After the meal the President produced two heavy wool blankets and spread them triumphantly in the shade of the car. In five minutes he was snoring. After he got to sleep I managed to swipe one blanket and snoozed myself, with the hum of insects in my ears.

It was near 4 o'clock when he awakened me. There he stood, fully clad for the stream—wearing my rubber boots!

The waders, half dried, hung from the big spruce like half a scarecrow. He said:

"I felt sort of conscience-stricken about those waders. Here it is the last day and you haven't had a chance to use 'em. You take 'em."

We went fishing. This time together and downstream. Downstream while the sun dipped lower, the river grew louder, the air chillier. Downstream beyond the rocky stretches to where the holes were really deep. Wet fly water it was and the browns began to hit with considerable zest when the sun was definitely under the horizon.

I was soaked to the waist in no time. The President, by canny manipulation, managed to stay dry even in the boots—no mean feat on the Brule. His 9-foot rod with the foot-long cork handle gave him casting distance where I was stymied with my eight-foot rod. He reached into places I couldn't touch.

He took browns. Always we take browns on the last day. Not a rainbow in the stretch. Nor a brookie. But browns, zippy, sparkling devils from the big lake, feeling again the frigid waters of the Bois Brule as they work upstream to spawn, later in the fall.

We were two miles from the car when the President called a halt. We clomped back along the bank, feeling our way in the gathering darkness. Twice we waded the river on short-cuts. Each time the cold river stung into me through those miserable waders.

At the car the President proceeded with the vespers of the Old Duck Hunters', Inc. He rubbed the back of his hand across his mouth and said: "Ah—smack!" He fumbled in the glove compartment, came up with a bottle and poured a drink apiece. After an interval he poured another.

Always there are two drinks. Never more except on special

occasions. We sat on the running board and sipped. Gradually there spread through my chilled body a warmer, kindlier feeling toward my fellowman.

I looked down at the waders. The toes were practically worn through. All the seams were either loose or frankly open. The surface was speckled with black rubber patches. At the crotch the outside material was rubbed away to the rubber beneath.

I must have shivered in the cool night breeze for the President poured a third drink. An unexpected gratuity. The President peered into my creel and opined I had caught the best mess of trout. He slapped me on the back and said I was a good fellow. There was about him a hail-fellow note that ordinarily he did not waste on me. He spoke:

"I'm glad I let you use those waders today. They sure are swell waders. I never wore a finer pair in my life. I want you to know just how I feel about them. I'd just as soon part with my wife as I would with those waders, they're that comfortable."

At the moment everything he said sounded logical. I looked again at the shredded waders. I said sure, they were great waders. I said I'd patch 'em and they'd do just fine for another season.

"By all means," said the President. "You'll need those waders next spring. I think you ought to have them. It's only right. Tell you what. I'll make you a deal. Duck season is comin' on and I need a pair of rubber boots like these."

I listened with interest. I was in a mood to say yes to almost anything this great and good fisherman would propose. He leaned toward me with fatherly affection and said:

"I'll swap you the waders for the boots!"

One of Gordon MacQuarrie's greatest stories
lies ahead. In it, he goes alone to spend three
weeks in his cabin.

There is a very grim reason why these
weeks are spent without his beloved Mr.
President. But he neither suggests it nor asks
in any way that you share the grief he carries.

Only at the story's end does he hint at his
loneliness and sorrow. "Surely, I was among
the most favored of all mankind," he cries.
"Where could there possibly be a world as fine
as this?" It is the ancient bitter question of
men who have no choice but to go on.
MacQuarrie goes on. Death has placed an even
higher value on life. His time alone is spent
in a frantic effort to live it to the fullest.

He tells himself, "There is much to be said in
favor of the solitary way of fishing and hunting.
It lets people get acquainted with themselves.
Do not feel sorry for the man on his own."

He says this because Mr. President is dead.
Hizzoner will come to the cabin no more.
He has gone to find if there is indeed another
world as fine as this. MacQuarrie fights to
understand and accept the crushing fact. To
sustain himself he turns back to the simple,
natural things he understands so well and
expresses it all in this memorable passage:

"You cannot shoot a pine knot or eat it, but
it is a lovely thing and makes a fire that
will burn the bottom out of a stove if you
are not careful. . . . Once I gave an artist a sack
of pine knots and he refused to burn them and
rubbed and polished them into wondrous
birdlike forms and many called them art.
Me, I just burn them. Until you have your
woodshed awash with pine knots, you have
not ever been really rich."

16

Nothing to Do
For Three Weeks

I left long before daylight, alone but not lonely. Sunday-morning stillness filled the big city. It was so quiet that I heard the whistle of duck wings as I unlocked the car door. They would be ducks leaving Lake Michigan. A fine sound, that, early of a morning. Wild ducks flying above the tall apartments and the sprawling factories in the dark, and below them people still asleep, who knew not that these wild kindred were up and about early for their breakfast.

The wingbeats I chose to accept as a good omen. And why not? Three weeks of doing what I wished to do lay before me. It was the best time, the beginning of the last week in October. In the partridge woods I would pluck at the sleeve of reluctant Indian summer, and from a duck blind four hundred miles to the north I would watch winter make its first dash south on a northwest wind.

I drove through sleeping Milwaukee. I thought how fine it would be if, throughout the year, the season would hang on dead center, as it often does in Wisconsin in late October and early November. Then one may expect a little of everything—a bit of summer, a time of falling leaves, and finally that initial climatic threat of winter to quicken the heart of a duck hunter, namely me.

To be sure, these are mere hunter's dreams of perpetual paradise. But we all do it. And, anyway, isn't it fine to go

on that early start, the car carefully packed, the day all to
yourself to do with as you choose?

On the highway I had eyes only for my own brethren of
the varnished stock, the dead-grass skiff, the far-going boots.
Cars with hunting-capped men and cars with dimly outlined
retrievers in back seats flashed by me. I had agreed with
myself not to go fast. The day was too fine to mar with haste.
Every minute of it was to be tasted and enjoyed, and remembered for another, duller day. Twenty miles out of the big
city a hunter with two beagles set off across a field toward a
wood. For the next ten miles I was with him in the cover
beyond the farmhouse and up the hill.

Most of that still, sunny Sunday I went past farms and
through cities, and over the hills and down into the valleys,
and when I hit the fire-lane road out of Loretta-Draper I
was getting along on my way. This is superb country for
deer and partridge, but I did not see many of the latter; this
was a year of the few, not the many. Where one of the
branches of the surging Chippewa crosses the road I stopped
and flushed mallards out of tall grass. On Clam Lake, at the
end of the fire lane, there was an appropriate knot of bluebills.

The sun was selling nothing but pure gold when I rolled
up and down the hills of the Namakagon Lake country.
Thence up the blacktop from Cable to the turnoff at Drum-
mond, and from there straight west through those tremendous
stands of jack pine. Then I broke the rule of the day. I hurried a little. I wanted to use the daylight. I turned in at the
mailboxes and went along the back road to the nameless
turn-in—so crooked and therefore charming.

Old Sun was still shining on the top logs of the cabin. The
yard was afloat with scrub oak leaves, for a wind to blow
them off into the lake must be a good one. Usually it just
skims the ridgepole and goes its way. Inside the cabin was
the familiar smell of native Wisconsin white cedar logs. I lit
the fireplace and then unloaded the car. It was near dark

when all the gear was in, and I pondered the virtues of broiled ham steak and baking powder biscuits to go with it.

I was home, all right. I have another home, said to be much nicer. But this is the talk of persons who like cities and, in some cases, actually fear the woods.

There is no feeling like that first wave of affection which sweeps in when a man comes to a house and knows it is home. The logs, the beams, the popple kindling snapping under the maple logs in the fireplace. It was after dark when I had eaten the ham and the hot biscuits, these last dunked in maple sirup from a grove just three miles across the lake as the crow flies and ten miles by road.

When a man is alone, he gets things done. So many men alone in the brush get along with themselves because it takes most of their time to do for themselves. No dallying over division of labor, no hesitancy at tackling a job.

There is much to be said in behalf of the solitary way of fishing and hunting. It lets people get acquainted with themselves. Do not feel sorry for the man on his own. If he is one who plunges into all sorts of work, if he does not dawdle, if he does not dwell upon his aloneness, he will get many things done and have a fine time doing them.

After the dishes I put in some licks at puttering. Fifty very-well-cared-for decoys for diving ducks and mallards came out of their brown sacks and stood anchor-cord inspection. They had been made decent with touchup paint months before. A couple of 12-gauge guns got a pat or two with an oily rag. The contents of two shell boxes were sorted and segregated. Isn't it a caution how shells get mixed up? I use nothing but 12-gauge shells. Riding herd on more than one gauge would, I fear, baffle me completely.

I love to tinker with gear. It's almost as much fun as using it. Shipshape is the phrase. And it has got to be done continuously, otherwise order will be replaced by disorder, and possibly mild-to-acute chaos.

There is a school which holds that the hunting man with the rickety gun and the out-at-elbows jacket gets the game. Those who say this are fools or mountebanks. One missing top button on a hunting jacket can make a man miserable on a cold, windy day. The only use for a rickety shotgun is to blow somebody to hell and gone.

I dragged a skiff down the hill to the beach, screwed the motor to it, loaded in the decoys, and did not forget to toss in an old shell box for a blind seat and an ax for making a blind. I also inspected the night and found it good. It was not duck weather, but out there in the dark an occasional bluebill skirled.

I went back up the hill and brought in fireplace wood. I was glad it was not cold enough to start the space heater. Some of those maple chunks from my woodpile came from the same sugar bush across the lake that supplied the hot biscuit sirup. It's nice to feel at home in such a country.

How would you like to hole up in a country where you could choose, as you fell asleep, between duck hunting and partridge hunting, between small-mouths on a good river like the St. Croix or trout on another good one like the Brule, or between muskie fishing on the Chippewa flowage or cisco dipping in the dark for the fun of it? Or, if the mood came over you, just a spell of tramping around on deer trails with a hand ax and a gunnysack, knocking highly flammable pine knots out of trees that have lain on the ground for seventy years? I've had good times in this country doing nothing more adventurous than filling a pail with blueberries or a couple of pails with wild cranberries.

If you have read thus far and have gathered that this fellow MacQuarrie is a pretty cozy fellow for himself in the bush, you are positively correct. Before I left on this trip the boss, himself a product of this same part of Wisconsin and jealous as hell of my three-week hunting debauch, allowed, "Nothing to do for three weeks, eh?" Him I know good. He'd have given quite a bit to be going along.

Nothing to do for three weeks! He knows better. He's been there, and busier than a one-armed paperhanger.

Around bedtime I found a seam rip in a favorite pair of thick doeskin gloves. Sewing it up, I felt like Robinson Crusoe, but Rob never had it that good. In the Old Duck Hunters we have a philosophy: When you go to the bush, you go there to smooth it, and not to rough it.

And so to bed under the watchful presence of the little alarm clock that has run faithfully for twenty years, but only when it is laid on its face. One red blanket was enough. There was an owl hooting, maybe two wrangling. You can never be sure where an owl is, or how far away, or how many. The fireplace wheezed and made settling noises. Almost asleep, I made up my mind to omit the ducks until some weather got made up. Tomorrow I'd hit the tote roads for partridge. Those partridge took some doing. In the low years they never disappear completely, but they require some tall walking, and singles are the common thing.

No hunting jacket on that clear, warm day. Not even a sleeveless game carrier. Just shells in the pockets, a fat ham sandwich, and Bailey Sweet apples stuck into odd corners. My game carrier was a cord with which to tie birds to my belt. The best way to do it is to forget the cord is there until it is needed; otherwise the Almighty may see you with that cord in your greediness and decide you are tempting Providence and show you nary a feather all the day long.

By early afternoon I had walked up seven birds and killed two, pretty good for me. Walking back to the cabin, I sort of uncoiled. You can sure get wound up walking up partridge. I uncoiled some more out on the lake that afternoon building three blinds, in just the right places for expected winds.

This first day was also the time of the great pine-knot

strike. I came upon them not far from a thoroughfare empty-
ing the lake, beside rotted logs of lumbering days. Those logs
had been left there by rearing crews after the lake level had
been dropped to fill the river. It often happens. Then the
rivermen don't bother to roll stranded logs into the water
when it's hard work.

You cannot shoot a pine knot, or eat it, but it is a lovely
thing and makes a fire that will burn the bottom out of a
stove if you are not careful. Burning pine knots smell as fine
as the South's pungent lightwood. Once I gave an artist a
sack of pine knots and he refused to burn them and rubbed
and polished them into wondrous birdlike forms, and many
called them art. Me, I just pick them up and burn them.

Until you have your woodshed awash with pine knots, you
have not ever been really rich. By that evening I had made
seven two-mile round trips with the boat and I estimated I
had almost two tons of pine knots. In even the very best
pine-knot country, such as this was, that is a tremendous haul
for one day; in fact, I felt vulgarly rich. To top it off, I dug
up two husky boom chains, discovered only because a link or
two appeared above ground. They are mementos of the logging days. One of those chains was partly buried in the roots
of a white birch some fifty years old.

No one had to sing lullabies to me that second night. The
next day I drove eighteen miles to the quaggy edge of the
Totogatic flowage and killed four woodcock. Nobody up
there hunts them much. Some people living right on the
flowage asked me what they were.

An evening rite each day was to listen to weather reports
on the radio. I was impatient for the duck blind, but this
was Indian summer and I used it up, every bit of it. I used
every day for what it was best suited. Can anyone do better?

The third day I drove thirty-five miles to the lower Douglas
County Brule and tried for one big rainbow, with, of course,
salmon eggs and a Colorado spinner. I never got a strike, but

I love that river. That night, on Island Lake, eight miles from my place, Louis Eschrich and I dip-netted some eating ciscoes near the shore, where they had moved in at dark to spawn among roots of drowned jack pines.

There is immense satisfaction in being busy. Around the cabin there were incessant chores that please the hands and rest the brain. Idiot work, my wife calls it. I cannot get enough of it. Perhaps I should have been a day laborer. I split maple and Norway pine chunks for the fireplace and kitchen range. This is work fit for any king. You see the piles grow, and indeed the man who splits his own wood warms himself twice.

On Thursday along came Tony Burmek, Hayward guide. He had a grand idea. The big crappies were biting in deep water on the Chippewa flowage. There'd be nothing to it. No, we wouldn't bother fishing muskies, just get twenty-five of those crappies apiece. Nary a crappie touched our minnows, and after several hours of it I gave up, but not Tony. He put me on an island where I tossed out half a dozen black-duck decoys and shot three mallards.

When I scooted back northward that night, the roadside trees were tossing. First good wind of the week. Instead of going down with the sun, Old Wind had risen, and it was from the right quarter, northwest. The radio confirmed it, said there'd be snow flurries. Going to bed that windy night, I detected another dividend of doing nothing—some slack in the waistline of my pants. You ever get that fit feeling as your belly shrinks and your hands get callused?

By rising time of Friday morning the weatherman was a merchant of proven mendacity. The upper pines were lashing and roaring. This was the day! In that northwest blast the best blind was a mile run with the outboard. Only after I had left the protecting high hill did I realize the full strength of the wind. Following waves came over the transom.

Before full light I had forty bluebill and canvasback decoys tossing off a stubby point and eleven black-duck blocks anchored in the lee of the point. I had lost the twelfth black-duck booster somewhere, and a good thing. We of the Old Duck Hunters have a superstition that any decoy spread should add up to an odd number.

Plenty of ducks moved. I had the entire lake to myself, but that is not unusual in the Far North. Hours passed and nothing moved in. I remained long after I knew they were not going to decoy. All they had in mind was sheltered water.

Next time you get into a big blow like that, watch them head for the lee shore. This morning many of them were flying north, facing the wind. I think they can spot lee shores easier that way, and certainly they can land in such waters easily. In the early afternoon, when I picked up, the north shore of my lake—seldom used by ducks because it lacks food —held hundreds of divers.

Sure, I could have redeployed those blocks and got some shooting. But it wasn't that urgent. The morning had told me that they were in, and there was a day called tomorrow to be savored. No use to live it up all at once.

Because I had become a pine-knot millionaire, I did not start the big space heater that night. It's really living when you can afford to heat a 20-by-30-foot living room, a kitchen, and a bedroom with a fireplace full of pine knots.

The wind died in the night and by morning it was smitten-cold. What wind persisted was still northwest. I shoved off the loaded boat. Maybe by now those newcomers had rested. Maybe they'd move to feed. Same blind, same old familiar tactics, but this time it took twice as long to make the spread because the decoy cords were frozen.

A band of bluebills came slashing toward me. How fine and brave they are, flying in their tight little formations! They skirted the edge of the decoys, swung off, came back again and circled in back of me, then skidded in, landing gear down. It was so simple to take two. A single drake mallard investigated the big black cork duck decoys and found out what they were. A little color in the bag looks nice.

I was watching a dozen divers, redheads maybe, when a slower flight movement caught my eye. Coming dead in were eleven geese, blues, I knew at once. I don't know what ever became of those redheads. Geese are an extra dividend on this lake. Blues fly over it by the thousand, but it is not goose-hunting country. I like to think those eleven big black cork decoys caught their fancy this time. At twenty-five yards the No. 6's were more than enough. Two of the geese made a fine weight in the hand, and geese are always big guys when one has had his eyes geared for ducks.

The cold water stung my hands as I picked up. Why does a numb, cold finger seem to hurt so much if you bang it accidentally? The mittens felt good. I got back to my beach in time for the prudent duck hunter's greatest solace, a second breakfast. But first I stood on the lakeshore for a bit and watched the ducks, mostly divers, bluebills predominating, some redheads and enough regal canvasback to make tomorrow promise new interest. The storm had really brought them down from Canada. I was lucky. Two more weeks with nothing to do.

Nothing to do, you say? Where'd I get those rough and callused hands? The windburned face? The slack in my pants? Two more weeks of it. . . . Surely, I was among the most favored of all mankind. Where could there possibly be a world as fine as this?

I walked up the hill, a pine-knot millionaire, for that second breakfast.

MacQuarrie now speaks eloquently and deeply about life. Not just with words; what takes place is equally significant.

After the death of Mr. President, the aging writer (he is 55) hunts and fishes alone. He travels widely in his job. The remembrance of his companion is tucked away. For several years, years filled with other writing, there are no more stories of the Old Duck Hunters' Association although the magazines urged him to continue the popular series. How could there be more stories? The President is dead.

17

Then a man comes along, a grinning man. He sneaks MacQuarrie a note at a crowded meeting. It has a familiar ring. "I've been reading your drivel for years," it says. "See me after school if you want to get some good partridge hunting." The bylaws are dusted off. The gavel falls. The Old Duck Hunters' Association, Incorrigible is called to order for the purpose of reorganization.

Most men never meet—much less befriend— someone who loves life. Chance thrust Mac- Quarrie into his first great friendship. Chance now thrusts him into his second and by so doing teaches the writer that the Old Duck Hunters' Association did not depend on a single individual, but on sustaining elements of life. The ability to extract the finest from it.

The Old Brown Mackinaw

When the President of the Old Duck Hunters' Association, Inc., died, the hearts of many men fell to the ground.

There was no one like Mister President. When the old-timers go there is no bringing them back, nor is there any hope of replacing them. They are gone, and there is a void and for many, many years I knew the void would never be filled, for this paragon of the duck blinds and the trout streams had been the companion of my heart's desire for almost 20 years.

I made the common mistake. I looked for another, exactly like Hizzoner. How foolish it is, as foolish as it is for a man to try to find another beloved hunting dog, exactly like the one that's gone.

In the years after Mister President's death I fished and hunted more than before, and often alone. There was a great deal of fishing and hunting, from Florida to Alaska, before a man came along who fit the role once occupied by Mister President. This is how it was:

I was sitting in the ballroom of the Loraine Hotel in Madison, Wisconsin, covering the proceedings of the unique Wisconsin Conservation Congress. I became aware that a man carrying one of the 71 labels for the 71 counties of the state was eyeing me.

He held aloft the cardboard label "Iowa" signifying that he was a Big Wheel in conservation from that western Wis-

193

consin county. He looked like Huckleberry Finn and he grinned eternally. One of the first thoughts I had about him was that he probably could not turn down the corners of his lips if he wanted to.

Each time I glanced at him his eye was upon me. This sort of thing is unnerving. Once he caught my eye and held it and grinned harder. I grinned back, foolishly. The beggar burst out laughing. I felt like a fool. He knew it and laughed at me.

Let me give you the picture more completely. In that room sat more than 300 dedicated, articulate conservationists. They were framing, no less, the fish and game code of this sovereign state for an entire year. Not in silence, you may be sure.

Up at the front table on the platform, as chairman of the Congress, sat Dr. Hugo Schneider of Wausau, with a gavel in one hand and—so help me!—a muzzle-loading squirrel rifle in the other. Each time Robert's Rules of Order seemed about to go out the window, Doc would abandon the gavel and reach for the rifle.

In this delightful pandemonium, in this convention of impassioned hunters and fishers and amidst the shrieks from the wounded and dying delegates, Wisconsin evolves its game and fish laws. And if you can think of a more democratic way, suggest it. We may try it.

At one point in the milling commotion and confusion, I saw my grinning friend slip to the floor and on his hands and knees start crawling toward me. By this manner of loco-motion he managed to evade the baleful eye and subsequent vengeance of Dr. Schneider, and he crawled up to my chair and handed me a scribbled note. Then still on his hands and knees, he crawled away. The note read:

> I've been reading your drivel for years. See
> me after school if you want to get some good
> partridge hunting.
>   Harry

Since then I suppose I've "seen him" a thousand times—on trout streams, on lakes, in partridge cover, in the deer woods, in the quail thickets, and yes, in the August cow pastures where the blackberries grow as long as your thumb, and in the good September days when you can fill a bushel basket with hickory nuts beneath one tree.

No outdoor event of its season escapes Harry. He is lean and fiftyish. He is a superb shot. He ties his own flies, one a black killer with a tiny spinner at the eye made from special light material he begs, or steals from dentist friends. On a dare, once he shinnied up a 12-foot pole and came back down head first. Once he made me a pair of buckskin pants. All in all, an unbelievable person.

How natural then, just this last October, that we should rendezvous, not in Iowa County—we save those partridge until December—but at the ancient headquarters of the Old Duck Hunters' Association, two whoops and a holler north of Hayward, Wisconsin.

I got there first. This is not hard for me to do when going to this place. Some things do not change and this is one of those things. It's exactly like it was before the atomic age. On that particular day, late October's yellow shafts were slanting through the Norways on the old cedar logs of the place. A chipmunk which had learned to beg in summer came tentatively close, then scurried away, uncertain now.

All was in order, down to the new windowpane I had to put in where a partridge in the crazy time had flown through. The label was still pasted to the tiny square of glass. I must scratch it off some day but there is always so much to do at places like this.

I went to the shed at the rear to check decoy cords and anchors. When you open this shed door one of the first things to catch your eye is a brown, checked-pattern mackinaw, about 50 years old, I guess. It belonged to the President of the Old Duck Hunters. I like to keep it there. It belongs there.

Flying squirrels had filled one pocket of the mackinaw with acorns. They always do that, but these avian rodents, so quick to unravel soft, new wool for nests, have never chewed at the threadbare carcass of Mister President's heroic jacket. Perhaps this is because the wool, felted and tough, has lost its softness and flavor.

I launched a boat, readied a smaller skiff and screwed the motor on the big boat. I fetched three bags of decoys down the hill and placed them handy. I put an ax—for blind building—in the boat with other gear, and when I got back up the hill to the cabin Harry was there.

On the way—a 300-mile drive—he had hesitated, he said, long enough to slay two pheasant roosters.

"I see," he said, "that you have been here an hour and have killed 'ary a duck or partridge." He explained that he had felt my auto radiator—"She's cooled only about an hour." This man operates like a house detective. I explained that in the remaining hour and a half of daylight I would prepare him a kingly supper.

"An hour and a half of daylight!" He flung two skinned pheasants at me, dashed to his car and returned, running, bearing fishing tackle.

"D'ja soak the boat?" he cried as he passed me. I doubt if he heard my answer for he was soon down the hill and nearing the beach when I replied. Within two minutes he was trolling.

The man never lived who could fill up each moment of a day like this one. Nor was there ever a one who could, once the day was done, fall asleep so fast. He goes, I am sure, into a world of dreams, there to continue the pursuits of fish and game, man's life's blood—well, his, anyway.

I lit the fireplace. No need for the big steel stove, or was there? Late October weather in the north can be treacherous.

I laid the big stove fire, to play safe. The provident Harry had made getting supper easy. You take two pheasants and cut them up. You save the giblets. You steam some wild rice for an hour. . . .

It was long after dark when Harry returned. He had a 7- or 8-pound northern and a walleye half as big—"If we're gonna be here for four days, somebody around here has got to bring home the grub."

I set the table fast for fear he would fall asleep. He stuffed himself with pheasant and wild rice and mentioned that he must not forget to tell his wife how badly I treated him. Then he collapsed on the davenport before the fire, and in one yawn and a short whistle he was gone. I washed the dishes.

No, he is not a shirker. Before sleep afflicts him he will kill himself at any job which needs doing, especially if it pertains to hunting and fishing. To prove his willingness for the menial tasks, I recall a deer camp one night when one of the boys brought in a 300-pound bear—dragged him right through the door and dropped him at Harry's feet.

Harry was wiping the dishes, clad only in a suit of new, red underwear. He had sworn to be the first man in that camp to bring in important game, and because now he obviously had not, he turned, dishcloth in hand, eyed the bear casually and remarked:

"Johnny, that's a mighty nice little woodchuck you got there."

Even when I turned on the radio for a weather report he did not awaken. His snores, wondrously inventive, competed with the welcome report of changing and colder weather. Outside the wind was coming along a bit and it was in the northwest. But mostly it was the warm wind hurrying back south ahead of something colder at its back.

Iowa County's nonpareil was bedded down in the far room

where his snores joined the issue with the rising wind which keened over the roof. A good fair contest, that.

When I arose I had to light the big heater for the weather had made up its mind. No snow, but a thermometer at 26 degrees and a buster of a wind. I hurried with breakfast because I thought we might have to build a blind on Posey's point. That point, the right one on this day, had not been hunted in the season. When I mentioned the reason for haste he explained:

"Man, I built that blind yesterday. You think I fooled away three hours just catching a couple fish?"

It is not possible to dislike a man like that. Furthermore, I knew this blind would be no wild dove's nest, but a thing of perfection, perfectly blended with the shore line.

A lot of people in this country think the Old Duck Hunters are crazy when they hunt this lake. We carry so many decoys that we have to tow them behind in a skiff. Fifty is our minimum, half of them over-sized balsas, and a scattering of some beat-up antiques more than 120 years old, just for luck.

Settling himself for some duck blind gossip, Harry began, "I was down on the Mississippi at Ferryville last week. Mallards all over the—".

"Mark!"

A hundred bluebills, maybe twice that, who knows, came straight in without once swinging, and sat. We never touched a feather as they rose. I have done it before and I'll do it again and may God have mercy on my soul.

"This," said Harry, "will become one of the greatest lies in history when I tell my grandchildren about it. I am reminded of Mark Twain. When Albert Bigelow Paine was writing his biography and taking copious notes, he once remarked to Twain that his experiences and adventures were wonderful copy.

" 'Yes, yes,' replied Mr. Clemens. 'And the most remarkable thing about it is that half of them are true.' "

He then set his jaw and announced he would kill the next three straight with as many shots. This he did, for I did not fire. While I was retrieving them in the decoy skiff, another bundle of bluebills tried to join those giant decoys and were frightened off by me. Walking to the blind from the boat, I saw Harry kill a canvasback.

He was through for the day and not a half hour had passed. Many Badgers will remember that late October day. Ducks flew like crazy from the Kakagon sloughs of Lake Superior to sprawling Horicon marsh, 300 miles away. Only one other day of that season beat it—Wednesday, November 2.

Harry cased his gun and watched. I cannot shoot like Harry, but getting four ducks on such a day was child's play. Many times we had more divers over our decoys than we had decoys. It was pick-and-choose duck hunting. I settled for four bullneck canvasbacks.

Back at the cabin we nailed their bills to the shed wall, and over a cup of coffee Harry said the divers we'd seen reminded him of the "kin to can't day." Then, he explained, the law let a man shoot the whole day through from as soon "as he kin see until the time that he can't see." I knew a place, Oscar Ruprecht's sugar bush, and we drove the eight miles to it.

This chunk of maple is on an island of heavier soil in an ocean of glacial sand, grown to pines. If its owner had the equipment he could tap 5,000 trees. Many know it and hunt it. We separated, for we are both snap shooters, or think we are.

The plan was to meet on a high, rocky bluff where the river Ounce passes by below, on its way to the Totagatic. Here was no dish like that easy duck blind venture. These were mature, hunted ruffed grouse, all the more nervous because the wind was high. On one of the tote trails where Oscar's tractor hauls the sap tank I missed my first bird, then missed two more.

A half mile to my right two calculated shots sounded, well spaced. Perhaps a double. Ah, well . . . My fourth bird was as good as dead when it got out of the red clover in mid-trail and flew straight down the road. I missed him, too.

Three times more, and later a couple more times Harry's gun sounded. Then two birds flung themselves out of the yellow bracken beside the two-rut road and I got one. When I was walking over to pick it up, a third pumped up and I got it.

It was noon when I got to the high bluff. Deer hunters with scopes on their rifles love this place. From it they over-look almost a half mile of good deer country in three direc-tions. My sandwich tasted good. I lit a little friendship fire and thought about other days on the river below me. It's a pretty good trout stream for anyone who will walk in two miles before starting to fish.

Harry came along. He'd been far up the valley of the Ounce, bucking fierce cover—no sugar bush tote trails in there, only deer trails. But he had five grouse. We hunted back to the car, and in his presence I was lucky enough to kill my third bird.

It was around 2 p. m. when we pulled into the cabin. My Huckleberry Finn who I have seen, on occasion, whittle away at a pine stick for 20 minutes without doing anything but meditate, was a ball of fire on this day. He tied into the ducks and partridge. When he had finished cleaning them his insatiable eye fell upon the woodpile.

You can spot those real country-raised boys every time when they grab an ax. They know what to do with it. No false moves. No glancing blows. In no time he had half a cord of fine stuff split and piled for the kitchen range and he went on from that to the sheer labor of splitting big maple logs with a wedge for the fireplace.

He spotted my canoe and considered painting it, but decided it was too cold, and anyway, it had begun to snow a little. Then he speculated about the weather, and when I said I wished I had a weather vane on the ridgepole, he went into action.

He whittled out an arrow from an old shingle, loosely nailed it to a stick, climbed to the roof and nailed it there firmly. I suppose that if I had mentioned building an addition to the back porch he'd have started right in. He came down from the roof covered with snow and said he wished he hadn't killed those four ducks in the morning, so he could go again.

"But, let's go anyway," he suggested. "No guns. Put out the decoys and just watch 'em."

Out there on the point the divers were riding that wind out of Canada. Scores of them rode into and above the decoys. Posey, the owner of the point, came along for a visit and decided we were both crazy when he saw what we were doing. Nevertheless, we had him ducking down as excited as we were when a new band of bluebills burst out of the snow. Only in the big duck years can a hunter enjoy such madness.

Our shore duty at dark that night involved careful preparations against the storm. We pulled up the boat and skiff higher than usual and covered everything with a weighted tarp.

Walking up the hill, I considered how nice it was to have one of the faithful, like Harry, on the premises. He should have been bone tired. Certainly I was. But before I relit the big heater he took down its 15 feet of stovepipe, shook out the soot and wired it back to the ceiling. He carried in enough wood for the remaining three days, stamping off snow and whistling and remembering such tales as one hears in all properly managed hunting camps.

He spied a seam rip in my buckskin pants and ordered me to take them off. While he mended them he complained bit-

terly about such neglect on my part—"There's nothing wrong
with the workmanship on these pants."

He had made them himself, two months before, from two
big chrome-tanned doeskins. He just walked into my house
one night with a gunny sack containing the skins, a piece of
chalk and some old shears his wife used for trimming plants.
He cut the pants out, fitted them to me and took them to the
shoemaker's shop where he sewed them up and affixed buttons. I never in my life wore pants that fit so well.

This man should have been born in the same time as a Kit
Carson or a Jim Bridger. Turn him loose anywhere in his
native heath, which is Wisconsin, and, given matches, an ax,
a fishhook and some string, he'll never go hungry or cold.

He is a true countryman, a species almost extinct. Each
day of the year finds him outdoors for at least a little while.
In trout season he hits the nearby streams for an hour or two
around sunup. His garden is huge and productive. In the
raspberry season you may not go near his home without being
forced, at gun point if need be, to eat a quart of raspberries
with cream.

He represents something almost gone from our midst. He
knows the value of working with his own hands, of being
eternally busy, except when sleeping. His last act that snowy
evening was to go to his car and return with a bushel of
hickory nuts. He set up a nut-cracking factory on a table,
using a little round steel anvil he had brought for busting
'em. He had a pint of hickory nut meats when I put the grub
on the table.

He almost fell asleep at the table. Then he yawned and
whistled and looked out the door and said he was glad it was
snowing hard—"Don't shoot at anything but cans in the
morning." He flopped on the davenport and was gone to
that far-off land where no trout of less than 5 pounds comes
to a surface fly and the duck season runs all year.

I tidied up and washed the dishes. I smelled the weather and smoked a pipe. The fireplace light danced on the big yellow cedar beams. The snow hissed against the window. The President of the Old Duck Hunters' Association should have been there.

Maybe he was. At any rate, I went out to the shed and took the old brown mackinaw off its nail and brought it in and laid it over Harry's shoulders. It looked just fine there.

*The Old Duck Hunters sally forth. Their
antics start anew. The new Mr. President is
more imaginative and inventive than the old.
More gastronomically inclined, perhaps, but
the familiar kindness and decency are there,
familiarly concealed behind outrageous insults
and pranks. And there is the same rich enjoyment of life and filling it with pleasure
and delight.*

*In one fabulous sequence from another story,
Mr. President leads a nature study group
through the woods, picking up deer droppings
and popping them into his mouth. He chews
each with great gusto and explains how
delicious they are. "Got three people to try
'em today," he confides to the junior member
gleefully. He explains also that previous to
the stroll he has carefully placed small, round,
black licorice balls among the deer leavings
which, of course, he was eating.*

*Remember the former Mr. President telling
the stranger the sunken barrel blinds were
porcupine traps, and he better be careful
around the secret place? Inc. still stands for
incorrigible.*

*The writer is now 56 years old. It will be
the last year of his life. This Indian summer
was to pluck at his sleeve and whisper, "Get
ready, my friend. I am just brushing by to
settle the dust and wash away today's
dead spent-wings."*

18

In Quest of the Saber-Toothed Cottontail

The President of the Old Duck Hunters' Association was picking raspberries in his cool garden when I drove my car up the steep driveway near the end of a stifling summer day. He assessed me:

"Of all the sunburned, dirty-faced, chigger-bit—!" He directed his voice toward the door just behind the grapevine which screened the kitchen porch. "Laura, I've got a bum out here. Shall I put him to work on the woodpile?"

I'd been up since 4 a.m., exploring the excellent smallmouth streams of southwest Wisconsin. In the last 40 miles I had gone like the homing pigeon to its cote, straight to the castle —aye, the oasis, the ever-normal hospice—of Harry J. Nohr, Mineral Point postmaster and President of the Old Duck Hunters' Association.

Laura appeared. Her welcome was drowned by the uproar of the two fixture-dogs of the Nohr demesne, Becky, a springer, and Bob, a shorthair. They sniffed and wagged. A third dog, looking not unlike a startled fawn, affirmed the barkings of her two comrades, but gently, almost timidly, as befits a lady.

"That there dog," Harry explained, "is Tina. She is a

Norwegian dog. Her owners are on a long vacation and we are teaching her to speak English and answer the telephone— just like Becky and Bob."

I persuaded Tina to accept me as a friend, but this she did tentatively. There was a vast difference between her and the two permanent and rowdy Nohr dogs. She was distant and gentle and she maintained an air of perpetual surprise, as if everything she encountered were brand new. When she reached out a paw it was like being touched by a feather. She was black with a hint of deep brown in her coat. She might have been a cocker if her legs were not so long.

"We have reason to believe," Harry explained, "that Tina is the daughter of an Irish water spaniel and a black cocker. It is true that she acts like she 'yust came over,' but who are we to ask questions? For all I know, her ancestors were at Valley Forge."

I got cleaned up, was overwhelmed with kindness and made sodden with food, and when the night came down Mister President and I sat on the back porch behind the grapevine and listened to the nighthawks and the turning of the spheres in their courses.

About curfew time Becky and Bob suddenly came to life and darted, barking, toward the four-foot woven garden fence. Tina hung back and added approving, but barely audible, barks to the joyous clamor at the fence.

"It's our rabbit," Hizzoner explained. "He lives in the garden. When Becky and Bob hear him, or smell him, they go for him. . . . I shall have to lower my voice so that Tina doesn't hear me. I do not want to hurt Tina's feelings." He leaned closer and whispered:

"Tina is afraid of rabbits. The only thing Tina is not afraid of is food. She's got a choke-bore nose and she's as strong as a horse, but she has decided to let others get excited about life. Maybe Becky and Bob will change her, but I don't think so."

He explained that Tina was the only Norwegian he had ever seen who was afraid of anything, and he deplored the circumstances which found him giving Tina bed and board because—"With only Becky and Bob to feed there were times when I thought I'd have to sell the post office to pay the horse meat bill."

We went to bed on the sleeping porch. The cool night breeze blew across the beds, and the President of the ODHA regaled as follows:

"That rabbit in the garden . . . his mother brought him here when he was little enough to squeeze through the mesh. She pushed him inside.

"It must have been like falling into heaven for that little rabbit. In a month he was bigger than his mother. And why not, boarding in the finest garden in southwest Wisconsin? His mother came every night to see how he was getting along, and he would push carrots through the fence for her. One night I caught him giving her an American Beauty rose and had to speak to him sharply, even if he was kind to his mother.

"Then we got Tina. Well, you saw Becky and Bob swearing at the rabbit, and you saw Tina hanging back. Tina may need a psychiatrist, possibly even a husband.

"However, don't give Tina too much the worst of it. That cottontail in the garden is no common, mine-run rabbit. He is the greater saber-toothed cottontail, found only in Iowa County, Wisconsin, a creature with the heart of a lion and the tushes of a wild boar.

"You may well ask why I have not driven the rabbit from my garden. Frankly, I am a little bit afraid of him. However, if he turns vicious I can always get some of the boys in the National Guard to bring up a field piece."

That is what the President of the Old Duck Hunters said. That and more, but I fell asleep listening to his voice, and so cannot report what must have been the purest of imagery, because he gets better, the more he talks. In no time the martins were on the wing outside the window in their matutinal rites, and not long after, fed, rested and stimulated, I departed.

Summer diminished. At frequent and well-timed intervals I returned to Hizzoner's domain to catch smallmouths, to stalk big brown trout on dark nights, to gather the wild blackberry, the wild plum, the wilder hickory nut and the much wilder ruffed grouse and bobwhite quail which inhabit Wisconsin's western counties.

On all of these expeditions we took Tina with us. And of course Becky and Bob. You are required to take Becky and Bob because if you do not they will set fire to the house.

Everything happened to Tina. She got stung by hornets and obtained commiserations—even homage—from Becky and Bob. She got lost when she was farther than 100 yards from Harry. She stepped on most of the sandburs in Iowa County. She got chased ignominiously by the white-faced and black Angus cattle, peaceful critters of the pastures who would not dare to trifle with the likes of Becky and Bob.

Watching Tina in the company of Becky and Bob, I concluded that the latter two were convinced that Tina, though one of them, was not of them. They treated her with respect and devotion. When they were hunting—and a fine working team they are—Tina did not enter into their considerations. While they hunted, Tina remained at heel.

"Tina," Harry explained, "is above hunting. She dwells in her own world. If she were a bee she would be the queen." It must be reported that she was a fetching-looking mutt, with black curly bangs and deep brown eyes which were either pools of uncalculated wisdom or the windows of an empty soul. To this day I can't say which.

Tina retained that look of perpetual surprise. Or was it mere aloofness from a world which she seemed to enjoy, but to which she chose to contribute nothing? Superbly equipped for water work, she would have none of it. She never fought with the town dogs; in fact, never needed to, for they left her alone. Becky and Bob, on the other hand, were valiant and free-swinging in passages at arms with their fellow citizens, of which Mineral Point has more than its share.

Not ever did I see Tina evince the least interest in a ruffed grouse, a duck or a rabbit, though one day she saw Mister President and me—reveling in the fleshpots of the Iowa County grouse pockets—kill five apiece, par for the course. That was all right with Tina. She was happy to be along with us—"Just don't ask me to take part in this horrid business," said her eyes.

Autumn dwelt long in the western hills and we of the Old Duck Hunters made the most of it. We went north for ducks at just the right time, late October and early November. We went north again in late November, and Hizzoner slew a great stag in a stand of snowy spruce and, upon arrival home, when challenged by the police chief as to his luck, explained that he had brought home only one, though he had killed several others. All this was duly published in the *Iowa County Democrat*, a newspaper of infinite understanding.

December stalked over the limestone hill country, and from time to time Mister President reported to me that he was carrying out the lodge rites by successful harassment of the rabbits, aided, of course, by Becky and Bob. No word about Tina. Perhaps she had been restored to the bosom of her family.

I discovered otherwise on New Year's Day, 1956. When I drove up the steep driveway, Becky and Bob rushed for the car. Tina, as befit one of her remote dignity, remained seated on the porch, a black, inscrutable sphinx. The plot called for a rabbit hunt, but there were amenities to be observed.

"After all," said Mister President, "This is New Year's Day and a time to celebrate with good food and large talk.

Furthermore, we are going to hunt the greater saber-toothed cottontail and we must be fortified."

The entrée was roast Muscovy duck, but there was also cranberry sauce, mashed potatoes, two kinds of salad, Christmas cookies, fruit cake, fudge, saffron cake, many kinds of jam, popcorn balls, taffy, jelly beans—and cherry pie.

It was to be, Hizzoner informed me, an all-out expedition against the fearsome sabertooth. It certainly was. When he lifted the first barbed-wire strand and commanded me to crawl under, four big chunks of Laura Nohr's fudge fell out of my pocket.

"Whatever you do," Hizzoner whispered, "don't miss the first shot. The sabertooth is like the Kodiak bear. You've got to anchor him with the first shot."

He popped a piece of fudge into his mouth and recalled one day "in these very same fields when Harold Pittz of Dodgeville got mauled by a sabertooth—had an awful time stopping the bleeding."

I loosened my belt and we moved forward, behind Becky and Bob. Harry continued:

"Us White Hunters out here on the Iowa County veldt have got to be careful with our customers. In case a sabertooth charges, you get behind me, if I ain't already up a tree."

In a dense patch of cover, Becky and Bob evinced profound interest, and Mister President whispered, "Watch it now. This is close quarters."

He kicked a brush pile and a cardinal flew out. I relieved my own tension by taking a bite out of a duck wing I had fetched from the Nohr table.

Down a long draw, through three more fences, and two more mouthfuls of duck wing, we came to what Hizzoner described as "a dead forest—notice how dark and eerie it is." Becky drove out a lone, hightailing cottontail. There was no chance for a shot. Harry remarked:

"That was a sabertooth. If there'd been only one of us he'd have charged."

A covey of quail flushed. Becky and Bob will hunt anything in which they think Harry is interested, and that is the way it should be with the dog of the true country man, who takes all the seasons as they come.

In the bottoms of some of the steeper hollows the going got pretty rough, but Hizzoner said he thought we could make it, as long as the jelly beans and chocolate turtles held out. In one thick cover the two dogs stirred up a pair of cottontails, and as they scuttled over a hill, unscathed, Harry cried:

"Thank heaven! They're running the other way."

Night came along and there was a spit of snow. On the way back to the car Harry showed me innumerable sabertooth tracks—"Just look at them, twice as big as elephant tracks. Some folks claim they're the tracks of the broad-clippered wowser, but I know better."

Driving homeward, he dwelt at length on the pleasures and challenges of hunting the saber-toothed cottontail, and also of the victuals awaiting us. "If I'm real nice to Laura and hang my hunting coat in the garage, she may make us some hot biscuits."

It was dark as the car went up the driveway. Becky and Bob were alert on the back seat. They knew they were home and it was just a question with Bob if he could get out of the car without getting nipped. Becky stood closest to the left rear door. She knew this was the one Harry would unlatch. The latch clicked, Becky butted open the door with her head, jumped out and awaited the emergence of her lord and master, teeth bared. She must have given poor Bob an especially nasty nip because he yipped and pursued her, promising vengeance.

They circled the house, both barking, Becky 15 feet ahead, but sometimes slackening up a bit so that Bob would be encouraged to continue the chase. The uproar brought

Laura to the kitchen door. Harry explained, rather elaborately and transparently, I thought, that he was "just about to hang my jacket in the garage, and thought you might whip up some hot biscuits for two starving big-game hunters." She promised she would and added, "See if you can find Tina. I haven't seen her all afternoon, and you know she never leaves the yard."

I helped Mister President search the yard. We called and whistled, and cased the yards of a few neighbors. Then Harry swung open the garage door and switched on the light, and that is where Tina was.

Tina the inscrutable, Tina the queenly, lay in a corner of the garage on a heap of old carpets. She was not alone. Six smaller Tinas had arrived some time during the afternoon and were safely and hungrily in Tina's charge.

As for Tina, she wore that same look of perpetual surprise. Mister President said he was not completely surprised, nor was he entirely prepared for the blessed event. He laid a gentle hand on Tina's dark head and sized up her family.

"They are," he announced, "unquestionably the children of Bob. Look at the brown color. Far as I can determine, they're all ladies, like their mother."

Becky and Bob, their feud temporarily ended, came into the garage. Tina's passive manner vanished and she snarled at them, ears back, teeth flashing.

"That's a hell of a way for a wife to greet her husband— and at a time like this," said Mister President. He comforted Tina and remade her bed and built a wall of boxes around her, stretching more old carpets over them to keep out drafts. Then he closed the garage door.

"She'll be warm enough there for the time," he said. "Six more mouths to feed. Now I will have to sell the post office. Give them away? Man, I can't give away my own flesh and blood!"

The biscuits were coming out of the oven as we walked

into the kitchen. The President of the Old Duck Hunters told Laura the Great News and she was pleased no end and had to go at once and see the puppies, after which two Old Duck Hunters assumed positions at the table and cleaned up the last of the Muscovy duck, the cranberry sauce, the Christmas cookies, the fruit cake, the saffron cake, the many kinds of jam—and the cherry pie.

This is the last Old Duck Hunter story. It was published after the author's death. Prophetically, in it Mr. President demands some guarantees from the man up above that he will provide some trout and bass water, "yes, and some first-rate grouse cover, and some duck hunting."

"What are you going to do if the Sickle Man tells you he will not bargain?" MacQuarrie asks.

"In that case," snaps back Mr. President, "I ain't going."

No one knew better than MacQuarrie the futility of bargaining with the Sickle Man. No one knew better than he that his beloved woods and waters must someday be left behind. That is why he made so very much of them while he was here.

19

You Can't
Take It With You

The President of the Old Duck Hunters' Association finished his repast that Sabbath noon and his wife reminded him that the lawn needed mowing, one martin house had been tilted by the wind and the garden clamored to be weeded.

Mister President walked through the summer kitchen which held a freeze box of treasure, including trout, bass and walleyes. His fishing jacket and tackle were in a neat pile by the door leading to the back porch where the wild grapevine twined. He eschewed it.

He strode out on the back porch and looked across the street at the United States post office where he was postmaster and where he often started working at 6 a. m. and remained until midnight. For the hundredth time he thought it might be a good idea to sell the post office, a drastic measure which he often expounded on opening days to customers who approved of the idea hilariously.

Bob, the shorthair, and Becky, the springer, galloped up and awaited the word from their lord and master. Perhaps they knew what was passing through his mind. Bob's tail was violently in favor of truancy, for Bob is a direct actionist. Becky, more the opportunist, merely sat and hoped for the best.

Mister President disappointed them both. He took the

lawn mower from the garage, lingering there only a few seconds to admire the sleek lines of a 16-foot canoe he was recovering with fiber glass. Within five minutes after the demon mower had begun to roar, three neighborhood urchins appeared from unknown crannies, looking for work, to which they were instantly put.

The three dandiprats, elevation about 40 inches, were signed on as horses, and Mister President explained that they were crossing the plains in a covered wagon and he was the wagon master.

"Gee-jap . . . steady . . . haw! Haw, you red-headed hoss! You wanna push the wagon and all our stores over the bank into the wide Missouri? . . . Steady . . . now, gee-jap."

The three hosses walked the mower up and down, halting occasionally on command of the wagon master to fall on their bellies and shoot it out with bands of Indian raiders.

A lady of considerable dignity, for such a pretty day, approached on the sidewalk.

"Sir!" She fixed the President with a fierce and righteous eye. "What do you mean by disturbing the Sabbath with this uproar?"

Heads poked cautiously out of nearby front doors and upper windows, for this lady was notorious in her determination to police the city of Mineral Point, Wisconsin, in the ways of Christianity as she saw them. The President of the Old Duck Hunters was not unequal to the occasion.

"Madam," he answered, "I plumb forgot it was Sunday, because I've been so damn busy minding my own business."

The lady went on her way, bloody, but unbowed, as screen doors closed softly and a little chorus of giggles floated from front porches beneath the 100-year-old elms. Above the roar of the mower, Mister President called out the marching orders:

"We'll make Alkali Bluff tonight, hosses. Plenty of grass and water for you there. Gee-jap."

The gallant hosses and/or Indian-fighting plainsmen had finished their strength-sapping labors and were ingesting fresh strawberries with thick cream—a quart apiece is the standard ration for all comers to this yard—when I drove my car up the short, steep driveway. The President flew into action.

"It's Geronimo and his band!" he cried. "Wheel the wagons into a circle and don't fire until you see the whites of their eyes."

The three plainsmen covered me with rifles that looked like Model 1873 Winchesters and fired white plastic balls. Mister President bravely directed the skirmish from behind a bowl of strawberries and cream—

"Shoot the hosses from under 'em, men. Then we'll tommyhawk 'em and scalp 'em when they're helpless on the ground!"

I advanced from my car waving a handkerchief on the middle section of a glass fly rod.

"Cease firing, men, the poor fellows are whupped."

Although I had recently dined, it was compulsory that I attack my portion of garden-fresh strawberries and cream. The three fighting men of the plains accepted additional helpings and sat there restuffing themselves, victorious and belching.

Mrs. President came out. She was about to cheer the billiard-table appearance of the lawn and saw me, so I had to accept another ladle of giant strawberries and impart the family news and amenities. Mister President volunteered:

"Now, Laura, he came all by himself all this way. Seems when I settle down to serious work somebody's always trying to lure me away."

The lady of his heart remarked that luring him away was about as difficult as persuading a rabbit to eat lettuce, and, for that matter, she would attend to the garden and straighten the martin house on its pole.

Mister President, by main force, imprisoned Becky and Bob in his own car to prevent them from following us, and as we backed down the driveway you could see them staring desperately at us through the rear window. At such a time you can hear a dog calling you unprintable names.

The smallmouth and trout domain we visited that day is part of the southwest corner of Wisconsin—the Driftless Area, as the geologists call it, where glaciers have never advanced or receded, and where a complete river system has been eroded by wind and rain and flowing water until the area is almost perfectly drained. A bucket of water thrown on the ground has only one way to go—downhill—looking for some other water.

In this land of the sky, so-called because hills are high and vistas are far, it has been estimated by Mister President that there are about a thousand miles of creeks and rivers which are predominantly smallmouth bass water, with some trout, especially browns in the upper reaches. I think his estimate is high but fear to challenge him, for he may add up that network of moving water to prove to me it's more than a thousand miles.

Our first stop was at the Fever River, not far from tiny Jenkinville. There we acquired a friend, Mr. Lyle "Fudge" Gates, straight as an arrow and merry as a meadowlark despite the burden of his 13 years. He was trying to catch a grasshopper and thus, eventually, a bass. In about four casts from the bank Mister President caught a 14-incher and presented it to Fudge with his compliments. Fudge took out for home on the dusty town road, clutching the giant to his ecstatic breast.

Gentlemen, I have had some awesome fishing in my time. I have stood on the big boulders alongside the Clearwater River not far from where it leaves Careen Lake, Saskatchewan, and found it almost impossible not to take two grayling on every cast. In that same province I have fished with four others and often all five of us have had on, simultaneously, northerns in the neighborhood of 20 pounds.

And that is fine, just fine. But let me vouchsafe that the pure delight imparted that day to Mr. Fudge Gates by Mister President, with a little black bass from a rather muddy little stream, was strangely satisfying, and appropriate.

At this place the Fever winds through closely cropped pastures holding dairy herds and beef cattle. Banks are trampled and those same banks fairly cry out for someone to come and plant cover on them. But the smallmouths are there. At least they are every time I attend to the local rites with Mister President.

Protocol while fishing with Hizzoner in his own domain demands the use of his tested, proven spinner fly—solid black dressing, red head, slim white rubber streamer tonguing out below the single hook. The spinner will twirl in the least of currents. It is made from a light, white metal used by dentists and it is begged, borrowed or stolen from them for this purpose by the President of the Old Duck Hunters.

I recommend that black spinner fly without reservation. I have seen it, in various sizes, take muskies, northerns, walleyes, trout and bass. Far as I know it is nameless. A more imaginative angler than I would likely have named it long ago. Hizzoner evolved it over a period of years, and if I may speculate about its effectiveness, I would guess that its chief attraction is in that spinner, which whirls like a dervish if you so much as blow on it.

It's a meat-in-the-pan fly-rod lure. Possibly there is something important in that solid black dressing. At any rate, one of the most successful of all the fly-rod men against the rainbows of the Douglas County Brule in Wisconsin was the late John Ziegler—and he put his faith in big, black bucktails.

Mister President, by his own admission, is a high-grader. He passes up a lot of water on those Driftless Area rivers. That means going from riffle to riffle and working the pools below the riffs. The process of high-grading brought a couple more smallmouths, and also Mr. Fudge Gates, who panted back to the streamside in time to get another bass a foot long and depart for home. We went along for the Grant River.

There's a place on this river where a gush of water leaps out of the limestone and falls 30 feet to the river. I stuck a thermometer into that flow and, though the air temperature was in the high 80's, the water was 54 degrees. It's colder than that in the ground, and that water, no doubt, is a solid reason why brother smallmouth tolerates the Driftless Area streams in spite of flash floods, silt and absence of bank cover.

It is surprising that so many miles of good smallmouth waters get so little pressure from anglers. The farmers in this opulent hill country hold down the bridges and the deep holes in an eternal quest for catfish. As for the bass angler, his work is easy. I wish it were harder, and it would be if those bald banks had only half the cover they need.

Mister President high-graded himself three more smallmouths within sight of that squirt of water from the limestone bluff above. He put them back, but said he'd save anything that got up to two pounds.

We moved along to the Platte River, to a place called King's Ford—high right bank, low left bank and the same surprisingly cold water from the limestone hill springs. Both of us picked up trout here—browns, ½-pounders—and these we saved. Like the bass, they were found in the holes below the riffs. They are not big enough to be called rapids.

On such days as this, the Old Duck Hunters are not averse to other charms of the Driftless Area. Short excursions into the box canyons along these valleys showed that the wild black raspberries were ripe and edible, that the blackberry crop would be a buster and that the wild grape tangles were bearing heavily after a year when the grapes were absent— and the ruffed grouse were not found at these favored tangles.

The area is dotted with wild crab apple trees. Each time I pass one I remember a day in brown October when the incorrigible Mister President paused before a tree loaded with red ripe crabs. He bit into one, smacked his lips, ate it, core and all.

"Honey crabs," he explained. "Sweetest apple this side of heaven."

Greedily I bit into one, though I should have known better. A more tasteless, a more bitter fruit has not touched the lips of man. How he ate one, for the sole purpose of getting a sucker like me merely to taste one, is something I shall never understand.

It was like chewing alum. And yet, Hizzoner, when he ate his, chewed and smacked and swallowed when his face should have been distorted and tears running down his cheeks. Hizzoner will go to great lengths for a laugh, but it takes a man of considerable will power to get 'em that way.

The Platte River was next, and when the dark began mounting up in the east we had two respectable smallmouths each, a brown trout each and some nice country to survey. We sat on a ledge of limestone and watched a farmer send his dog for the cows. A headstrong heifer sneaked away from the obedient herd, but her tawny nemesis brought her back with his teeth snapping close to her heels—"You do that again, sister, and I'll really bite you!"

No, not wilderness fishing. Not in the slightest. Pastoral is the word for it. No big fish to brag about. No heavy water to breast in waders. Just fishin' in nice country. The farmer whose dog rounded up the cows came over and sat on the limestone for a chat—

"I'll tell you, boys. You drop a good, stinky doughball into one of them holes and you're apt to get holt of the biggest dam' catfish this side the Mississippi."

It was all right with the Old Duck Hunters. Hizzoner

figured it as an even split—"They get the catfish and we have the fun."

Quail scuttled across the gravelly town road as we pulled out of there and Mister President spoke of autumn days. "The grouse'll concentrate around those grape tangles again, sure's you're born." A considerate conservation commission apportions to this area the longest ruffed grouse season in Wisconsin, extending from mid-October to a few days before Christmas. Forget it if you haven't got a dependable dog, or those hills will murder you.

Within about six miles from home Mister President surmised, "She's probably got the garden weeded and the martin house fixed and it's still early." It was early, for a fisherman, not much after dark. He directed me to drive through a long, two-gate lane. We parked at the end of it and walked about a quarter of a mile through deep grass to the headwaters of what can be nothing but a feeder of the Pecatonica River.

That is all I can say about this place. If it has a name, Hizzoner did not tell me, although I prodded him a few times, just gently. I have found it profitable not to attempt to trespass into the mind of a fisherman.

The stream here was slight, with little widespreads and like the others we had seen that day, largely devoid of bank cover. A fine place for the casting of the night line with a fly rod. Mister President vanished in the dark upstream, and I combed the nearby waters for almost an hour with no luck.

I was at the car waiting for him when he came through the high grass to the lane. He dropped a brown of about three pounds on the floor of the car. "There's browns in there big enough to swallow that one."

Becky and Bob began a two-dog riot when the car burst up the short, steep driveway. Hizzoner quieted them hurriedly. He opened the garden gate and made a swift appraisal. "Not a weed in sight," he whispered. He went to the martin house pole and squinted upward. "Straight as a string."

The back porch light flicked on and the Old Duck Hunters were summoned to sit at a table arranged there of fried chicken and fearsome quantities of strawberries. Any number of people who have been entrapped on that back porch in the strawberry season can testify that when they leave they can be picked up and bounced, like a basketball.

Hizzoner lay back in a porch chair and contemplated the night through the grapevine leaves. Becky and Bob came close, the better to adore him. He sighed.

"Laura," he said, "I can probably find time tomorrow after work to weed the garden and straighten the martin house."

She said, "Huh!" She added succinct and appropriate remarks, for the time was opportune, but I noticed that she mussed his hair and smiled the smile of a wise woman before she left us alone on the porch.

We spoke of the country we had seen. I suggested he should consider himself lucky to be living in the midst of it, but, said I, there would come a day when the old geezer with the big sickle would come along and put an end to our days.

Mister President, challenged, sat bolt upright in his chair.

"Let him come," said he. "I've got to have a guarantee from him that he's got some trout and bass water up there in the big yonder—yes, and some first-rate grouse cover and some duck hunting."

"You can't take it with you," I said, which was indeed the obvious reply to this man challenging fate. "Nor, can you send it on ahead. What are you going to do if the Sickle Man tells you he will not bargain?"

There was nothing obvious in the reply that the President of the Old Duck Hunters snapped at me.

"In that case, I ain't going."